33
THE SERIES™

AUTHENTIC MANHOOD™
MANHOOD

VOLUME **4**

TRAINING GUIDE

A **MAN** AND HIS **WORK**

A **MAN** AND HIS **WORK**

Published by Authentic Manhood • © 2014 Fellowship Associates Inc. • Reprinted November 2020

Project Management & Art Direction: Rachel Lindholm
Design: Samantha Corcoran, Mike Robinson, Details Communications, Lindsey Woodward
Editors: Rick Caldwell, Caroline Damron, Grant Edwards, Rachel Lindholm, Katie Ryburn, Steve Snider,
    Rebekah Wallace, Lindsey Woodward
Contributors: Hunter Beaumont, Mike Boschetti, Brian Goins, Tierce Green, Steve Snider, Josh Weiss

Authentic Manhood, Men's Fraternity, and 33 The Series are registered trademarks of Fellowship Associates Inc.

To order additional copies of this resource, go to AuthenticManhood.com, or contact LifeWay Resources online at LifeWay.com.

Printed in the United States of America

Distributed by:

Authentic Manhood
12115 Hinson Road, Suite 200
Little Rock, AR 72212

Groups Ministry Publishing
LifeWay Resources
One LifeWay Plaza
Nashville, TN 37234

TABLE of CONTENTS

04
intro
AUTHENTIC MANHOOD
How to Experience **33** as an Individual or Group
How to Make the Most of Your **33** Experience
From a Weekly Gathering to a Global Movement
A Movement that Grows Authentic Men and Plants Churches
The Presenters

09
session **one**
TENSION
Session Outline
Four Conventional Responses
Wealth, Power, and Recognition
THE RED ZONE: 10 Reasons Why People Hate Their Jobs

25
session **two**
BLUEPRINT
Session Outline
Biblical Blueprint
The Second Question Men Are Asked
THE RED ZONE: Created To Be A Giver

43
session **three**
COURAGE
Session Outline
Nehemiah: Creator and Cultivator
Converted Work
THE RED ZONE: Odd Jobs

57
session **four**
ESSENTIALS
Session Outline
10 Essentials
Resistance is a Reality
THE RED ZONE: Gospel Identity

73
session **five**
TRAPS
Session Outline
Wealth and Financial Health
Rethinking Retirement
THE RED ZONE: Statistics from the Workplace

91
session **six**
CATALYZERS
Session Outline
The Truth Behind The Catalyzers
Bless Your Community
THE RED ZONE: Well Said
Additional Resources
33 Action Plan
Answer Key

How to **Experience 33** as an **Individual** or **Group**

33 The Series can be viewed on DVD, downloaded from **authenticmanhood.com**, or experienced via mobile apps. Any of these three delivery systems can be utilized by groups or individuals. *One of the great things about this series is the variety of ways it can be used and/or presented.*

The series is organized in a way that provides flexibility and offers a variety of options on how the material can be experienced. *33* is organized into six topically-themed volumes that include six sessions each. *Volumes include topics on a man's design, story, traps, parenting, marriage, and career.* You can choose to commit to one volume/topic at a time, by limiting a particular experience to six sessions, or you can combine multiple volumes into one expanded experience that includes more sessions (12, 18, 24, 30, or 36). You can also choose any combination thereof.

However you choose to experience 33, the manhood principles and practical insights taught in each volume are essential for every man on the journey to Authentic Manhood. 33

How to Make the Most of **Your 33 Experience**

33 **The Series** *is more than just a video series for you to watch, and then mark off your list. When experienced with other men, it can be the pathway to Authentic Manhood that changes your life forever. Authentic Manhood is truly a movement that you can become a part of, and then passionately invite others to join.*

1 Make sure you have a team. Your experience will be greatly enhanced if you form a team with other men or at least one other man to help process the truths that you receive.

2 Make sure every man has a 33 Training Guide. A 33 Training Guide will enable men to take notes, record a strategic move after each session and create an action plan at the end. It also contains articles, interviews and features that will support the truths men receive from the video teaching.

3 Make sure you stay caught up. All the sessions of 33 can be purchased online and downloaded for only a few dollars per session. If you are viewing 33 with a group and miss a session, you can download the session you missed and stay caught up. (Purchase downloads at *www.33authentic.com*)

Most importantly...

4 Make sure you pass on the truths you learn to other men. When session six ends, the exciting part just begins. Don't just sit back and wait for another study. Instead step up and find another man or group of men to lead through the volume you just completed. For a small investment of just a few dollars, you can download your very own set of this series and use it to make a HUGE investment in the lives of other men.

From a **Weekly Gathering** to a **Global Movement**

Several years ago, Dr. Robert Lewis responded to the desire of a handful of men who were hungering for more than a Bible study. They wanted a map for manhood – a definition of what it meant to be a man. They needed help to leap over the hurdles they were encountering in life.

Robert responded by launching a weekly gathering called Men's Fraternity, challenging men to join him at six o'clock each Wednesday morning for 24-weeks. From the depth of his own personal experience and the pages of Scripture, Robert developed what came to be known as the Men's Fraternity series:

• *The Quest for Authentic Manhood*
• *Winning at Work & Home*
• *The Great Adventure*

What began with a few men huddling up grew into a weekly gathering of more than 300 men. In just a few years, local attendance at Men's Fraternity climbed to more than a 1,000 men.

The message of Authentic Manhood began to spread and soon exploded into a global movement *impacting more than a million men in more than 20,000 locations worldwide* – from locker rooms to boardrooms, from

churches to prisons, on military bases and the field of battle, at NASA and even on a space shuttle mission. Wherever the messages were heard, the challenge remained the same: to call men to step up and follow biblical manhood modeled by Jesus Christ.

The Men's Fraternity curriculum *was created on the front lines where men live, written in the trenches in response to men who pleaded for purpose and direction.* It has proven to be the most widely used and effective material on Authentic Manhood available today.

What began as a weekly meeting of men searching for answers to their manhood questions has grown into a bold movement that has dramatically impacted the lives of men, their families and communities. 33

A Movement that Grows Authentic Men and Plants Churches

For over a decade, Fellowship Associates has helped over *a million men all over the world to discover the life of truth, passion, and purpose they were created to live through Authentic Manhood materials*. During that same decade, Fellowship Associates has been directing a church planting residency program that has been recognized as one of the most effective church planting efforts in the world.

The proceeds from the sale of Authentic Manhood materials have helped underwrite the planting of 65 (and growing) gospel-centered churches throughout the United States as well as in Canada, Hong Kong, Dubai, Guatemala, Poland, and Spain. 33

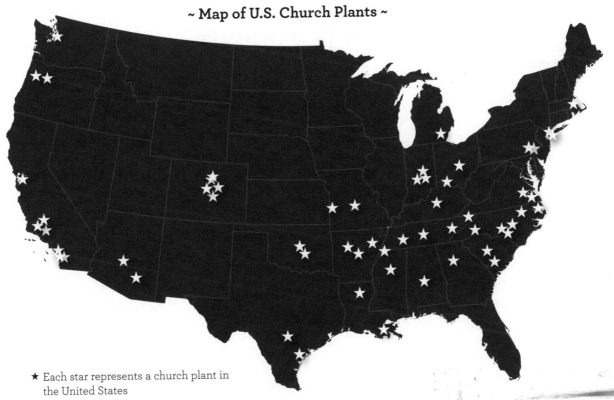

~ Map of U.S. Church Plants ~

★ Each star represents a church plant in the United States

The **Presenters**

BRYAN CARTER

Bryan Carter taught the original Men's Fraternity curriculum to a group of more than 800 men over a three-year period at Concord Church. Additionally, he has been a frequent speaker at local and international churches, conferences and events.

Bryan is the Senior Pastor of Concord Church in Dallas, Texas.

He is the author of a 28-day devotional book entitled *Great Expectations.* Bryan also contributed to the book *What Two White Men of God Learned from Black Men of God,* co-authored by Dr. Joel Gregory and Dr. Bill Crouch.

A recreational basketball player, Bryan is a fan of the NBA's Dallas Mavericks.

Bryan and his wife Stephanie are the parents of two daughters, Kaitlyn and Kennedy, and one son, Carson.

TIERCE GREEN

Tierce Green is Pastor of House Churches at Church Project in The Woodlands, Texas where his primary role is to call men up and equip them to lead and care for people. He also travels extensively as a speaker at conferences and training events. He taught the principles of Authentic Manhood to over a thousand men each week over a seven-year period in a seasonal gathering called The Quest.

Tierce created and produced a 12-session video series for men called *Fight Club: Some Things Are Worth Fighting For.* He has also written curriculum for Student Life and LifeWay.

A lifelong Dallas Cowboys fan, Tierce's favorite activities include landscaping, grilling just about anything, and having good conversations.

He and his wife Dana were married in 1987. They have one daughter, Anna.

JOHN BRYSON

Seeing firsthand the impact the original Men's Fraternity curriculum had on his own life, John Bryson decided to teach the material himself. In the years since, he has led thousands of men through the basic ideas of biblical manhood.

John is a co-founding teaching pastor of Fellowship Memphis in Memphis, Tennessee.

In 2010, he completed his Doctor of Ministry from Gordon-Conwell Theological Seminary. John is also the author of *College Ready,* a curriculum for college students, and travels the country consulting and investing in churches, church planters, leaders and new ideas.

A native of Harlan, Kentucky, John played baseball at Asbury College.

He and his wife Beth have 6 children: Brooke, Beck, Bo, Boss, Blair and Bayne.

Tension

SESSION **ONE** | Training Guide

Tension Presented by Bryan Carter

I. INTRODUCTION

1.   A Man and His Work

2.   Work is a _____ force in the life of every man creating tensions that must be balanced.

3.   Most of us have never engaged in a deliberate _____ that helps us reflect deeply on God's design and purpose for work.

4.   Work can be exhilarating, fulfilling and purposeful.

5.   We want to give a new _____ of the nature and purpose of work.

II. WHAT WE WANT FROM WORK

1.   We all want to be _____.

   •   We all want to be good at what we do for a living.

2.   We want to be fairly compensated for a job well done.

3.   We want the _____ job fit.

4.   We want to know our work matters.

   •   We want more than success, we our want work to be _____ and significant.

III. CONVENTIONAL RESPONSES TO WORK

1. Disengaged

    • _____ of American workers are either "not engaged" or "actively disengaged" at work.[1]

    • This misunderstanding has been robbing men of truth, passion and purpose ever since sin entered the world.

2. Disappointed

    • Less than half of U.S. workers report being _____ with their job; and a third are disappointed in the amount of money they earn and the amount of stress in their jobs. [2]

3. Over-engaged

    • 86% of American men report working more than 40 hours in a typical week[3] while taking fewer vacation days than people in most countries.[4]

    • Many men often over-engage in work because they are _____ it over everything else in life.

4. Underworking

    • This response often springs from a lack of personal ambition or career _____.

[1] "Majority of American Workers Not Engaged in Their Jobs," Gallup, 28 October 2011, *http://www.gallup.com/poll/150383/majority-american-workers-not-engaged-jobs.aspx.*
[2] "U.S. Workers Least Happy With Their Work Stress and Pay," Gallup, 12 November 2012, *http://www.gallup.com/poll/158723/workers-least-happy-work-stress-pay.aspx.*
[3] United Nations Statistics Division, "Percent Working More than 40 Hours Per Week," *http://data.un.org/Data.aspx?q=40&d=GenderStat&f=inID%3a119.*
[4] "Expedia® Vacation Deprivation® Key Statistics," Expedia®, *http://www.expedia.com/p/info-other/vacation_deprivation.htm*

IV. THE HISTORICAL ERAS OF WORK

1. Agricultural Era

    - The identity and value of a man was most often tied to his relationship with his _____ and his community rather than his work.

    - As late as 1890, 40% of the U.S. population still listed their occupation as farming.[5] Today, less than 1% of the U.S. population list their occupation as farming.[6]

2. Industrial Era

    - During the industrial era, we see an emphasis on efficiency and _____.

    - The mass production of the industrial era also enabled mass consumption.

    - Work became the _____ way men defined themselves.

Informational Era

    - This era is defined by the use of technology to replace workers and familiarity with technology is a minimal requirement for many jobs.

    - The informational era is defined by innovation.

V. TENSIONS FROM THE HISTORICAL ERAS OF WORK

1. Many of you are experiencing a real blurring between _____ and your work .

    - "In contemporary technological civilization, which can boast of remarkable labor-saving innovations, human beings paradoxically work more than they have ever worked before... Increasingly, people's lives today alternate between frenzied work and frenzied play. Rest has been driven out of leisure."
      - Miroslav Volf

[5] Ikerd, John, "New Farmers for a New Century." Presented at Youth in Agriculture Conference, Ulvik, Norway, 14-15 February, 2000. Available Online http://web.missouri.edu/ikerdj/papers/Newfarmer1.htm.
[6] U.S. Environmental Protection Agency, "Demographics," http://www.epa.gov/agriculture/ag101/demographics.html.

2. Another tension that many of you may feel is having to change jobs or careers multiple times.

    •   Change has become the _____ not the exception.

3. The potential for vocational _____ between fathers and sons.

    •   It is not as easy for a dad to be involved in a son's vocational development.

VI. CONCLUSION

1. We are going to take you through a _____ process and equip you with a God-sized vision of work.

2. We will show you God's orginal intention for work.

DISCUSSION / REFLECTION QUESTIONS

1. How does your job create tension in your life? Explain.

2. Bryan talked about four things all men want from work: success, fair compensation, a good fit, and meaning. Are any items on that list presently eluding you or creating frustration in your job?

3. Are you more prone to disengage, feel disappointed, over-engage, or underwork in your occupation? How have you tried to resist these conventional responses to work?

4. Bryan noted that during the informational age men have experienced a blurring between their work and leisure. He quoted one expert who stated that "people's lives today alternate between frenzied work and frenzied play. Rest has been driven out of leisure." Are there clear boundaries between your work and your leisure? How has the informational era created tensions in your work life?

5. How did your dad's view of work affect you? Was there ever any vocational tension between you and your parents?

RESOURCES ON THE FOLLOWING PAGES:

- The Four Conventional Responses (p. 16-17)

- Wealth, Power & Recognition (p. 18-21)

- **THE RED ZONE:** 10 Reasons People Hate Their Jobs (p. 22-23)

4 CONVENTIONAL RESPONSES TO WORK

- » Lack of contentment in a job

- » Unmet expectations

- » Death of a dream

- » Work feels like a deficit or dark cloud

DISAPPOINTED

- » Allowing your work to consume your time and thoughts

- » Can be considered a virtue by some

- » Can't relax without having work withdrawals

- » Make work a source of significance, worth or value

OVER-ENGAGED

- » Just going through the motions

- » Not passionate about what you're doing

- » Work is just a means to a paycheck

- » Ultimate goal is retirement

DISENGAGED

- » Do whatever it takes to avoid work

- » Leisure is main goal

- » No clear career vision, just dabble in different things

- » Better at intending to work than actually working

UNDERWORKING

EXPOSING
THE EMPTY PROMISES OF WORK

BY JOSH WEISS

Scripture is very clear; men were created to work. Work provides direction and allows us to use our talents and abilities to express ourselves and impact the world. From day one in Eden to day one hundred million in eternity, there has been and always will be work for us to do as image-bearers of God and co-creators with Him. Ultimately, to be made in the image of God is to be made in the image of a worker.

God has positioned each of us in the world and commanded us, as He did Adam, to "rule over and subdue the earth." The Creator of the universe has made us the steward of our own small piece of His kingdom and then charged us as men with the responsibility of not only preserving but prospering it. However, the reality is that we are fallen people living in a fallen world. Our sin has warped our attitude toward work. We struggle to see it as anything but a necessary evil, and the redemptive purpose behind our work is buried underneath the empty promises of **WEALTH, POWER,** and **RECOGNITION.** Work becomes something we do to provide for the parts of life we enjoy, to gain the approval of others or to feel in control. We are no longer motivated by God's idea of work but by whether or not our job meets our deepest needs. In essence, we have elevated work to a place it was never intended to be while simultaneously stripping it of all of its deeper, God-given meaning. The irony is astounding.

In *Mere Christianity*, C.S. Lewis writes, "Most people, if they had really learned to look into their own hearts, would know that they do want, and want acutely, something that cannot be had in this world. There are all sorts of things in this world that offer to give it to you, but they never quite keep their promise."[1] For most men, work is this thing Lewis speaks of, a thing that always over-promises and under-delivers.

These three promises of work mentioned above - the promises of **WEALTH, POWER,** and **RECOGNITION** - are not enough to satisfy, yet they dominate the marketplace. They are the motivations that wake us up in the morning, drive us during the day and always leave us unfulfilled as we lay our heads down at night. Yet, we continue to chase them, hoping tomorrow will be different, expecting different results from a recipe with all of the same ingredients. How do we get out of this "cul-de-sac of stupidity," as one pastor has called it? How do we free ourselves from this search for meaning?

We must expose these empty promises for what they are…

LIES.

WEALTH

THE LIE OF WEALTH tells us that if we just made more money, then we would be fulfilled. If we just made more money, we could be more comfortable at home, take better vacations, save more for retirement, retire earlier, etc. It tells us that our salary defines our value and beckons us to do whatever is necessary to increase it.

This lie runs rampant in our capitalist society where the sole goal of most men is to make as much money as possible as quickly as possible so they can retire as soon as possible, leading to over-worked men who spend the best hours of their days in the best years of their lives trying to increase the bottom-line instead of pouring time and resources into those they love and the world around them. It is a lie that may build a bank account but will never build a legacy.

We must see the incredible impact that a life invested can have. As I have heard it said, "You'll never see a hearse pulling a U-Haul." You cannot take it with you. There will come a day where we all meet death, the great equalizer, and, in that day, it will not matter how big our account balance is but how well we stewarded what was entrusted to us for the glory of God and the benefit of others.

POWER

Many men are also prone to believe **THE LIE OF POWER.** The lie of power offers true fulfillment when we are in control. These men take delight in the submission of others to their command. They say things like, "It's my way or the highway," or "If you don't like it, you can leave." They have no regard for the well-being of others; instead, they relish the opportunity to put someone in their place and show someone who is boss. This lust for power will eventually create a vicious tyrant who reigns supreme and whose very presence warns others that they dare not defy him. His wife cringes under his leadership, his children resent him, and his employees ask for a transfer.

Yet, the irony of it all is that any power we as humans may have is simply an illusion. There is not one of us who at any moment could not be stripped of everything for which we have so aggressively fought. It takes only a pebble thrown down from on high to topple the walls of our own weak, little kingdoms we try so desperately to defend.

RECOGNITION

Lastly, we as men may be motivated by recognition. **THE LIE OF RECOGNITION** tells us that fulfillment at work will come when people recognize our accomplishments. Once people see how well we do our job or how much work we do, then we will be appreciated. The lie of recognition tells us to ensure that we are visible, to elevate ourselves above others and to look out for ourselves first. Those who buy into the lie of recognition cannot be supportive of someone else's work because they view others as "the competition." They are always looking out for themselves because they are afraid that someone else might take their praise, or worse, their position.

The lie of recognition might be the most painful of all because it puts us on the treadmill of performing. We must recognize, as an authentic man, that meaning and fulfillment are not found in how well we compare to others but in what God has said about us when He showed His love and grace through His Son.

[1]C.S. Lewis, *Mere Christianity*, (New York: Scrivner, 1943), 104-105.

IT IS MY PRAYER

that we as men would not buy into these empty promises involving work but would, instead, be **MOTIVATED BY GOD'S GRACE**, what He's already done for us and His call to further the portion of His kingdom that He has already so graciously entrusted to us. Might we take Him at His word that our work matters regardless of how much **WEALTH**, **POWER**, or **RECOGNITION** we obtain. It matters because He promises us that, in Him, our labor is not in vain.

10 REASONS
PEOPLE HATE THEIR
JOBS

10- THEY THINK THE GRASS IS GREENER SOMEPLACE ELSE

9- THEIR VALUES DON'T ALIGN WITH THE COMPANY'S

8- THEY DON'T FEEL VALUED

7- JOB INSECURITY

6- THERE IS NO ROOM FOR ADVANCEMENT

5- THEY ARE UNHAPPY WITH THEIR PAY

4- THERE IS TOO MUCH RED TAPE

3- THEY ARE NOT BEING CHALLENGED

2- THE PASSION IS GONE

1- TERRIBLE BOSS

Ilya Pozin, "Top 10 Reasons People Hate Their Jobs: LinkedIn," *Huffington Post*, 7 July 2013. http://www.huffingtonpost.com/2013/07/11/why-people-hate-jobs_n_3579873.html

SUPPORTING RESOURCES

Volf, Miroslav. *Work in the Spirit: Toward a Theology of Work.* Wipf and Stock, 1991.
Miroslav Volf offers a theology of work. The first two chapters offer a very helpful discussion of the historical eras of work and how they have affected our contemporary world.

Nelson, Tom. *Work Matters: Connecting Sunday Worship to Monday Work.* Crossway, 2011.
Tom Nelson offers an easy-to-read perspective on why work is important. This book can help men trying to find the value of work amidst all the tension it creates.

The content in the resources above does not necessarily reflect the opinion of Authentic Manhood. Readers should utilize these resources but form their own opinions.

Blueprint

SESSION **TWO** | Training Guide

Blueprint Presented by Tierce Green

I. INTRODUCTION

1. This session will give you a God-inspired, gospel-centered vision for your work. We're calling it our Biblical _____ for work.

   See complete Blueprint on pages 34-35

2. We will answer three big questions:

   - What is work?

   - What are we to do in our work?

   - Who are we to be in our work?

II. BIBLICAL BLUEPRINT PART 1: WHAT IS WORK?

1. The conventional view of work is that it's just a _____, a paid position of regular employment.

   - It's just a job and a means to a paycheck.

   - The ultimate goal is retirement.

2. From God's perspective, work is more than just a job; it's a vocation.

   - A vocation is both _____ and purposeful.

     ○ It's personal: God calls every man to work. It's part of His plan for our lives.

     ○ It's purposeful: It's more than just an endless to-do list. It's participating in something God is doing in the world through us.

- "For we are [God's] workmanship, created in Christ Jesus for good works, which God prepared beforehand, that we should walk in them." Ephesians 2:10 (ESV)

- Work is so much more than just gainful employment or a necessary evil or only a means to paying the bills.

- A vocational perspective allows you to bring a totally different _____ to work. It reshapes everything you do in your work.

3. What is work? It's a vocation- God's personal and purposeful call on your life.

III. BIBLICAL BLUEPRINT PART 2: WHAT ARE WE TO DO IN WORK?

1. God Himself is a worker and He _____ work for mankind by creating and cultivating.

    - "In the beginning, God _____ the heavens and the earth."
      Genesis 1:1 (ESV)

    - God _____ His work by building an enviroment where it could flourish.

2. Mankind was made to _____ God's work by creating and cultivating and by helping develop God's world to its full potential.

    - "God created man in his own image, in the image of God he created him;... And God blessed [mankind]. And God said ... 'Be fruitful and multiply and fill the earth and subdue it and have dominion over the fish of the sea and over the birds of the heavens and over every living thing that moves on the earth."
      Genesis 1:27-28 (ESV)

- "The LORD God took the man and put him in the garden of Eden to work it and keep it." Genesis 2:15 (ESV)

3. God made _____ _____ over His creation to care for it, bring order to it, and develop it to its full potential for the benefit of mankind and for the glory of God.

   - "God left creation with deep untapped potential for cultivation that people were to unlock through their labor... [and] we are called to stand in for God here in the world exercising stewardship over the rest of creation in his place as his vice-regents. We share in doing the things that God has done in creation-- bringing order out of chaos, creatively building civilizations out of the material of physical and human nature, caring for all that God has made. This is a major part of what we were created to be... [Work] is rearranging the raw material of God's creation in such a way that it helps the world in general, and people in particular, thrive and flourish."[1] -Tim Keller

   - Our work is a way we can _____ the world and make it a better place.

   - Understanding work from God's perspective helps us to see how our work is a way we can develop the world and make it a better place in such a way that ultimately brings glory to the Creator of it all.

   - "Take the portion of my kingdom... I am making you my steward over your office, your workbench, your kitchen stove. Put your heart into mastering this part of my world. Get it in order; unearth its treasure; do all you can with it. ... We don't labor simply to survive, instincts do that... [instead] God has given each of us a portion of His kingdom to explore and develop to its fullness."[2]
   —Richard Pratt, *Designed for Dignity*

   - You can begin to live out this _____ of work right now.

4. Create and cultivate- that means using our God-given time, talents, and resources to bring things into existence and develop, order, and manage them for the benefit of mankind and for the _____ of God.

[1] Tim Keller, *Every Good Endeavor*, (New York: Dutton, 2012).
[2] Richard Pratt, *Designed for Dignity*, (Phillipsburg, NY: P&R Publishing, 1993).

IV. BIBLICAL BLUEPRINT PART 3: WHO ARE WE TO BE IN OUR WORK?

1. Jesus came to earth to save us and to be God's perfect _____
    to provide an example of how mankind is to engage in all of life, including our
    work life.

    - Through Jesus, we can be forgiven of all of our sins and adopted into God's
      family.

    - In His 33 years on earth, Jesus also gave us an _____ to follow, an
      inspiration for how we are to live.

      "Jesus as a matter of fact is a Brother to us as well as a Savior - an elder Brother
      whose steps we may follow. The imitation of Jesus has a fundamental place in
      the Christian life; it is perfectly correct to represent Him as our supreme and only
      perfect example."[3] - J. Gresham Machen

    - Jesus calls us to not only believe in Him, but also to _____ Him.

        ◦ "Go therefore and make disciples of all nations... teaching them to observe
          all that I have commanded you." Matthew 28:19-20 (ESV)

        ◦ "Whoever does not bear his own cross and come after me cannot be my
          disciple." Luke 14:27 (ESV)

        ◦ "Whoever says that he abides in [Jesus] ought to walk in the same way in
          which [Jesus] walked." 1 John 2:6 (ESV)

        ◦ "Look to Jesus, the author and perfecter of our faith." Hebrews 12:2

2. Jesus set the example for mankind by being a "_____ presence" in all
    areas of His life including His work.

    - Wherever Jesus went things got better and others flourished. Whatever He was
      doing, people experienced Him as a life-giving presence.

[3] J. Gresham Machen, *Christianity and Liberalism* (New York: Macmillan, 1923), 98 as quoted in Hood, *Imitating God*, 70.

- "'The first man Adam became a living being;' the last Adam, [Jesus], became a life-giving spirit." 1 Corinthians 15:45 (ESV)

- "It is more blessed to give than to receive." Acts 20:35 (ESV)

- Jesus said: "I came that they may have _____ and have it abundantly." John 10:10 (ESV)

- "Our model is the Jesus, not only the Jesus of Calvary, but the Jesus of the workshop, of the roads, and of the demands and oppositions."[4] - C.S. Lewis

3. Three powerful ways men can be a life-giving presence in their work:

    - Provision - provide for others

    - Attitude - have an attitude of _____

    - Excellence - perform our jobs with excellence

    - A Life-Giving Presence: being present, dependable, and excellent in our work with an attitude of humility for the benefit of others and for the glory of God.

[4] C. S. Lewis, *The Four Loves*, (Orlando: Harcourt Books, 1960), 6.

DISCUSSION / REFLECTION QUESTIONS

1. As you view your work as a vocation, not just a job, how would you explain it as both personal to you and purposeful as a part of God's bigger story?

2. What does it look like for you, whether your work is blue-collar or white-collar, to create and cultivate in your occupation? Discuss how both blue-collar and white-collar workers can follow the create and cultivate mandate.

3. J. Gresham Machen once said: "Jesus as a matter of fact is a Brother to us as well as a Savior—an elder Brother whose steps we may follow. The imitation of Jesus has a fundamental place in the Christian life; it is perfectly correct to represent Him as our supreme and only perfect example." Do you agree with this quote? If so, what does that mean for our lives as men?

4. Tierce mentioned three ways we can all be a life-giving presence in our work: provision, attitude, and excellence. Name some specific ways you can be a life-giving presence in your work.

RESOURCES ON THE FOLLOWING PAGES:

- Biblical Blueprint (p. 34-35)

- The Second Question Men Are Asked (p. 36-39)

- **THE RED ZONE:** Created to Be A Giver (p. 40-41)

THE **3** *parts of our*
BIBLICAL
BLUEPRINT
for WORK

1 WHAT IS WORK?
VOCATION

Work is more than just a job

IT'S PERSONAL:
- God's plan for your life
- Personal to your talents, gifting and season

IT'S PURPOSEFUL:
- Participating in something bigger that God is doing in the world through us
- Part of our personal story within God's story

WHAT DO WE DO?
CREATE & CULTIVATE

God modeled work for mankind by creating and cultivating for the benefit of others
- First, He created by bringing new things into existence
- Second, He cultivated His work by building an environment where it could flourish and commissioned Adam, His co-worker, to care for it alongside Him

God made man in His image to create, cultivate, and develop God's world
- In the very beginning work was given to mankind as a gift, not a curse, designed to be part of every man's story
- He gave us the privilege and responsibility to care for and develop the earth for the benefit of mankind and for His glory

WHO ARE WE TO BE?
A LIFE-GIVING PRESENCE

In addition to coming to earth to save us from our sins, He also came as an example to imitate
- We are called to follow Jesus

Jesus set the example of being a "life-giving presence" in all areas of His life, including work
- While Jesus was doing His work on earth, He blessed others. People experienced Him as a life-giving presence
- As we follow Him, we desire to be a life-giving presence in our work

The Second Question Men Are Asked

BY BRIAN GOINS

"What do you do?"

George usually answered this question following "What is your name?" upon take-off. Right after the attendant dropped off drinks in business class he'd turn to his seat-mate and say,

"International real estate."

"Wow," the fellow traveler would lean in, "Do you travel often?"

"Enough."

Enough to earn upgrades, a better than average living, and for George, to see that little rise of the eyebrow and hear the elevated pitch in their voice when people responded, "Oh, that must take you to some exciting places."

George loved that.

Or used to.

The real estate crash of 2008 grounded George Zaloom. Today, the Staten Island native lifts his eyes to the sky, spots the contrails of a jet, and reflects on the reality that he gives a different response to that second question these days.

George stands outside a two-bay garage. A blue and white sign advertises, "Zaloom's Auto Repair: Oil Changes. Tune Ups. Brakes. Shocks. State Inspections."

An air gun staccato breaks the rhythm of a hammer pounding on drums. A wrench clangs on the floor.

Before he brokered real estate deals all over the world, George had a knack for starting businesses. "But then everything fell apart. We lost everything. The only thing we had left was an automotive business we started years ago." He went from taking red-eyes to rotating tires.

At church the other day he was introduced to a friend's father who already knew the answer to the second question. He recognized his name and said,

"Oh, you're the mechanic."

When men ask the second question, "What do you do?," it's virtually impossible for us not to link our identity with our profession. George, like every man, enjoyed the respect he received when what he did impacted who he was in the eyes of people. And he knew the difference when one raised their eyebrows for an "investment banker" vs. "a mechanic."

"I find that people have expectations of mechanics," George speaks above the din, "that they are swindlers, cheats, and fool people into doing things that don't need to be done. We're trying to change that." For that to happen, George had to change his expectations.

Conventional wisdom says a job is simply a means to an end. Men use jobs to pay bills and pander their egos, earn retirement, and earn respect.

George knew both extremes; he had worked both white and blue collar jobs. But George realized that whether he was a mechanic, a real estate mogul, or even a monk... when you tie in your self-worth to your work, your joy sits on a susceptible fault line. A line that can quickly shift to downsizing, disability, or sudden downturns; you constantly battle insecurity or instability.

In the conventional work model, you work to prove you matter. You work to prove you are a somebody. Eventually, George realized he could work because he mattered to **SOMEBODY**, not because he needed to prove something. He started to understand what theologians term a "calling."

William Bennet, author of the anthology, *The Book of Man*, says:

"God didn't promise financial wealth, but he did promise joy.

I knew there had to be joy in this job. If I couldn't find it then there had to be something wrong. I could be in a prison in Iraq for preaching the gospel, but He has me here [for a reason]."

"Your 'calling' is your life's work. It can be done enthusiastically or carelessly, cheerfully or grudgingly.

Approached the right way, a man's labor can be both his vocation and his *avocation*. Done improperly, his work can be what philosopher Leo Strauss deemed a 'joyless quest for joy.' It's up to you. Your occupation can be a means to an end, or it can be an end in itself."[1]

Vocation comes from the Latin root, "to call." But for there to be a calling, there has to be a Caller. George started to realize, "this is where God has me. I've got to start changing my attitude."

Oliver Wendell Holmes said, "Every calling is great when greatly pursued."[2]

"I began to realize there was no separation between what I did at church and what I did at work," George admitted. "They were the same thing. I'm here to do His will, not my own. I really started liking it."

Where does He have **YOU**?

On March 18, 1968, a few weeks before he was assassinated, Martin Luther King Jr. spoke to a crowd of street sweepers in Memphis, Tennessee. He told them, "If it falls your lot to be a street sweeper, go on out and sweep streets like Michelangelo painted pictures; like Shakespeare wrote poetry; like Beethoven composed music; sweep streets so well that all the host of heaven and earth will have to pause and say, 'Here lived a great street sweeper, who swept his job well.'"[3]

George spies another jet zooming off on a familiar route. He doesn't mind answering the second question any longer. "I'm a mechanic," he proudly states. "For now, that's my calling." He walks back into the shop to answer a ringing phone, "It's a great day at Zaloom's. How can I help you?"

The story in this article is based off of, "This is Our City- Yes, I'm the Mechanic"
http://www.christianitytoday.com/thisisourcity/newyork/yes-im-mechanic.html
[1]William J. Bennett, *The Book of Man: Readings on the Path to Manhood* (Nash-

[2]Oliver Wendell Holmes, *Speeches by Oliver Wendell Holmes* (Boston: Little, Brown, and Company, 1900), 17.
[3]Martin Luther King, Jr, "The Three Dimensions of a Complete Life," in *A Knock at Midnight*, eds. Clayborne Carson and Pete Holloran

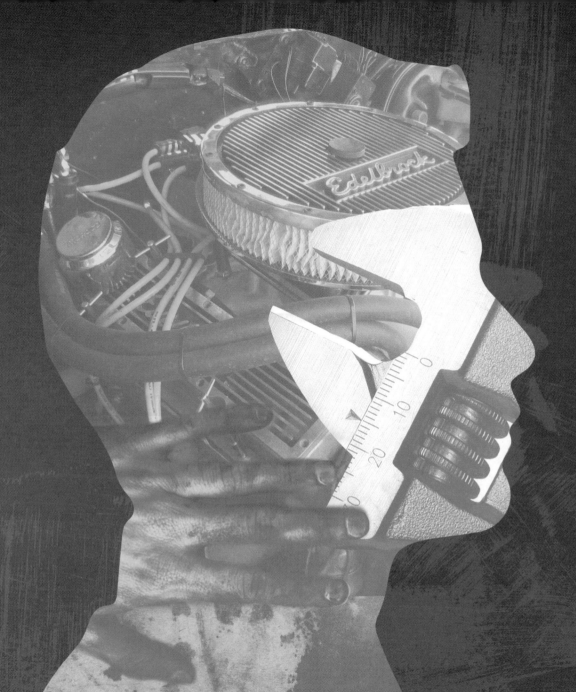

Back to work.

CREATED

In Matthew 6, Jesus asks, "Why would you store things up here where they will eventually fade away when you could store things in heaven that will last for eternity?"

Jesus' words revolutionize our work perspective. When God made man, He made him for more than chasing after the worldly pursuits of money and possessions; He made him to both provide and give...like He, Himself, did in creation and continues to do each day. God uses His possessions to provide for and bless us. Being made in His image, He intends for us to do the same.

God's word calls us to steward our resources wisely, to be givers and to bless others.

- "Do not lay up for yourselves treasures on earth, where moth and rust destroy and where thieves break in and steal." **Matthew 6:19-20 (ESV)**

- "But if anyone does not provide for his relatives, and especially for members of his household, he has denied the faith and is worse than an unbeliever." **1 Timothy 5:8 (ESV)**

- "Let the thief no longer steal, but rather let him labor doing honest work with his own hands, so that he may have something to share with anyone in need." **Ephesians 4:28 (ESV)**

- "If among you, one of your brothers should become poor... You shall open your hand to him and lend him sufficient for his need, whatever it may be... You shall give to him because for this the LORD your God will bless you in all your work and in all that you undertake." **Deuteronomy 15:7-8, 10 (ESV)**

- "In all things I have shown you that by working hard in this way we must help the weak and remember the words of the Lord Jesus, how he himself said, 'It is more blessed to give than receive.'" **Acts 20:35 (ESV)**

- "The point is this: whoever sows sparingly will also reap sparingly, and whoever sows bountifully will also reap bountifully. Each one must give as he has decided in his heart, not reluctantly or under compulsion, for God loves a cheerful giver." **2 Corinthians 9:6-7 (ESV)**

- "Honor the LORD with your wealth and with the firstfruits of all your produce; then your barns will be filled with plenty, and your vats will be bursting with wine." **Proverbs 3:9-10 (ESV)**

- "They are to do good, to be rich in good works, to be generous and ready to share, thus storing up treasure for themselves as a good foundation for the future, so that they may take hold of that which is truly life." **1 Timothy 6:18-19 (ESV)**

- "One gives freely, yet grows all the richer; another withholds what he should give, and only suffers want. Whoever brings blessing will be enriched and one who waters will himself be watered." **Proverbs 11:24-25 (ESV)**

to be a GIVER

SCRIPTURE REFERENCES

Genesis 1:1 (ESV) "In the beginning, God created the heavens and the earth."

Genesis 1:27–28 (ESV) "God created man in his own image, in the image of God he created him; ... And God blessed [mankind]. And God said ... 'Be fruitful and multiply and fill the earth and subdue it and have dominion over the fish of the sea and over the birds of the heavens and over every living thing that moves on the earth.'"

Genesis 2:15 (ESV) "The LORD God took the man and put him in the garden of Eden to work it and keep it."

Matthew 28:19–20 (ESV) "Go therefore and make disciples of all nations ... teaching them to observe all that I have commanded you."

Luke 14:27 (ESV) "Whoever does not bear his own cross and come after me cannot be my disciple."

John 10:10 (ESV) "... I came that they may have life and have it abundantly."

1 Corinthians 15:45 (ESV) "'The first man Adam became a living being;' the last Adam [Jesus] became a life-giving spirit."

Ephesians 2:10 (ESV) "For we are [God's] workmanship, created in Christ Jesus for good works, which God prepared beforehand, that we should walk in them."

Hebrews 12:2 (NASB) "[Look to] Jesus, the author and perfecter of our faith..."

1 John 2:6 (ESV) "Whoever says he abides in [Jesus] ought to walk in the same way in which [Jesus] walked."

SUPPORTING RESOURCES

Crouch, Andy. *Culture Making: Recovering Our Creative Calling.* IVP Books, 2008. Andy Crouch argues that Christians should not withdraw from the world but rather actively engage it by creating and cultivating. This a great book for those who want to learn more about how to create and cultivate in their jobs.

Hood, Jason. *Imitating God in Christ: Recapturing a Biblical Pattern.* IVP Academic, 2013. Scholar, Jason Hood, offers a convincing case that the imitation of Jesus is a key command of the New Testament and a trustworthy guide for how Christians should engage life.

Hunter, James Davison. *To Change the World: The Irony, Tragedy, and Possibility of Christianity in the Late Modern World.* Oxford University Press, USA, 2010. In this academic work, professor James Davison Hunter calls Christians to change the world by being a "faithful presence" in their spheres of influence—including their work.

The content in the resources above does not necessarily reflect that opinion of Authentic Manhood. Readers should utilize these resources but form their own opinions.

Courage

SESSION **THREE** | Training Guide

Courage Presented by John Bryson

I. INTRODUCTION

1. Create and Cultivate: Using our God-given time, talents, and resources to bring things into existence and develop, order, and manage them for the benefit of others and for the glory of God.

II. NEHEMIAH'S STORY- HOW TO CREATE AND CULTIVATE

1. Persia had _CONQUERED_ Israel and many Israelites lived as exiles there. Nehemiah, like many other Israelites, longed to return home to Israel one day to help restore and rebuild their nation.

    • Nehemiah held a _CUP BEARER_ position on the King's staff.

    • Nehemiah had a personal dream to use his talents to rebuild Israel.

    • "I took up the wine and gave it to the king. Now I had not been sad in his presence. And the king said to me, 'Why is your face sad, seeing you are not sick? This is nothing but sadness of the heart.' Then I was very much afraid. I said to the king...'Why should my face not be sad, when the city, the place of my fathers' graves, lies in ruins, and its gates have been destroyed by fire?' Then the king said to me, 'What are you requesting?' So I prayed to the God of heaven. And I said to the king, 'If it pleases the king, and if your servant has found favor in your sight,... send me to Judah, to the city of my fathers' graves, that I may rebuild it.'" Nehemiah 2:1-5 (ESV)

2. Nehemiah was a _CREATOR_.

    • "Nehemiah hoped to use his management skills to rebuild the walls of Jerusalem and reinstate stability so that economic and civic life could begin to flourish again in Israel." - Tim Keller[1]

    • First, notice that Nehemiah had a work-_VISION_ that blessed others.

[1]Tim Keller, *Every Good Endeavor*, (New York: Dutton, 2012), 120.

- Does your work-vision bring __LIFE__ to you, your family, your community and the world?

- Nehemiah courageously pursued his idea despite being afraid.

- Nehemiah turned to God in __PRAYER__. In the middle of his pitch to the king, he turned to God for help.

- Nehemiah also had a well-thought out work strategy.

  - "And the king said to me... 'How long will you be gone, and when will you return?' So it pleased the king to send me when I had given him a time. And I said to the king, 'If it pleases the king, let letters be given me to the govenors of the province Beyond the River, that they may let me pass through until I come to Judah, and a letter to Asaph, the keeper of the king's forest, that he may give me timber to make beams for the gates of the fortress of the temple, and for the wall of the city, and for the house that I shall occupy.' And the king granted me what I asked."
    Nehemiah 2:6-8 (ESV)

- Begin with the __END__ in mind.

- Four takeaways from Nehemiah "Creating":

  1. A work-vision that blesses others
  2. Courageous in the face of fear
  3. Depended on God in prayer
  4. A well-thought out strategy

  See Feature in Training Guide on pages 50-51

3. Nehemiah was a __CULTIVATOR__ in his work.

"So we labored at work, and half [of the men] held the spears from the break of dawn until the stars came out. I also said to the people at the time, 'Let every man and his servant pass the night within Jerusalem, that they may be a guard for us by night and may labor by day.' So neither I nor my brothers nor my servants nor the men of the guard who followed me, none of us took off our [work] clothes; [and] each kept his weapon at his right hand." Nehemiah 4:21-23 (ESV)

- All of us need to expect _OPPOSITION_ to come and be ready to make strategic adjustments.

- The importance of being willing to work hard.

- He took time to _REST_ and celebrate his accomplishments.

"And at the dedication of the wall of Jerusalem they sought the [priests] in all their places, to bring them to Jerusalem to celebrate the dedication with gladness, with thanksgivings and with singing... Then I brought the leaders of Judah up onto the wall and... [they] gave thanks... And they offered great sacrifices that day and rejoiced, for God had made them rejoice with great joy." - Nehemiah 12:27-43 (ESV)

- Three Takeaways from Nehemiah "Cultivating":

  1. Fought to overcome resistance
  2. Willing to work hard
  3. Took time to rest and celebrate

III. PAUL'S TEACHING - HOW TO BE A LIFE-GIVING PRESENCE

1. Once Paul started following Jesus, he was all about modeling Jesus' _LIFE GIVING_ spirit in his work.

   - Paul did a lot of blue-collar work.

     ° In Acts 18:3, we learn that Paul was a tentmaker - a man who worked with his hands.

   - "Be imitators of me, as I am of Christ." 1 Corinthians 11:1 (ESV)

2. Three ways to be a life-giving presence in our work:

1. Provide for __OURSELVES__ .

   - "If anyone is not willing to work, let him not eat. For we hear that some among you walk in idleness, not busy at work, but busybodies. Now such persons we command and encourage in the Lord Jesus Christ to do their work quietly and to earn their own living." 2 Thessalonians 3:10-12 (ESV)

2. Provide for our family.

   - "If anyone does not provide for his relatives, and especially for members of his household, he has denied the faith and is worse than an unbeliever."
                                                            1 Timothy 5:8 (ESV)

3. Give to those who are in __NEED__ .

   - "Let the thief no longer steal, but rather let him labor doing honest work with his own hands, so that he may have something to share with anyone in need."
                                                            Ephesians 4:28 (ESV)

   - Authentic Men are __GIVING__ men.

DISCUSSION / REFLECTION QUESTIONS

1. How do the stories and lessons of Nehemiah and Paul give you courage to live out our Biblical Blueprint for work?

UNDERSTAND OPPISITION IS PART OF WORK
GOD IS ALWAYS WITH YOU. WHAT IS YOUR
PURPOSE

2. In this session, we learned that Nehemiah was courageous in the face of fear. What fears are you currently experiencing in your work life? Nehemiah also pressed through resistance. Are you facing any resistance in your work?

CHANGE MARKS WORK, AND IS MOSTLY
RESISTED. MOST OF MY IDEAS ALWAYS
FACED OPPISITION

3. Nehemiah BOTH prayed and planned when contemplating a big career move. Are you more inclined to pray or plan when it comes to challenges in your work life? Why?

PLAN TWO OF MY WORST TRAITS WERE
PRIDE AND NO PATEENCE

4. Nehemiah allowed himself to dream big and trust God fully with his work-life. Do you give yourself permission to do that with yours? Why or why not?

LACK OF PATIENCE NOT HEARING
I ALWAYS HAD MY OWN PLANS

RESOURCES ON THE FOLLOWING PAGES:

- Nehemiah: Creator and Cultivator (p. 50-51)

- Converted Work (p. 52-53)

- THE RED ZONE: Odd Jobs (p. 54-55)

CREATOR
CULTIVA

WE LEARNED IN THIS SESSION THAT NEHEMIAH MADE THE BOLD DECISION TO TRANSITION FROM A HIGHLY-COVETED AND DISTINGUISHED POSITION ON THE KING'S STAFF—HE SERVED AS THE KING'S CUP-BEARER—TO PURSUE A DIFFERENT VOCATION THAT WAS NEAR AND DEAR TO HIS HEART.

REMEMBER, DEEP IN NEHEMIAH'S HEART, he felt God had given him a dream. He had a personal desire to use his talents and resources to return to the land of Israel and help rebuild its capital city, Jerusalem, which was in shambles after being conquered. This vision prompted a career change for Nehemiah.

He left his stable position as a government official, and became an urban planner and developer in order to help rebuild his hometown.[1] Within his job as a developer, he gives us a powerful Biblical example of a man living out the second part of our Biblical Blueprint—to create and cultivate in our work for God's glory. There are several steps he took and choices he made that we can learn from and apply to our own work as we create and cultivate in our own vocations.

TOR

KEY STEPS AND CHOICES THAT HELPED NEHEMIAH

CREATE

 &

CULTIVATE

- He had a work-vision that included blessing others
- He had courage in pursuit of the vision
- He had a dependence on God in prayer
- He had a well-thought out strategy

- He fought to overcome resistance
- He was willing to work hard
- He took time to rest & celebrate his accomplishments

CONVERTED WORK

BY HUNTER BEAUMONT

Why do you work? Why do you work hard? **If you're one of the "driven" types, why are you so motivated?** Why do you care about advancing in your field, climbing the corporate ladder, growing your business, getting the next promotion, developing the new product?

Our answers to these questions reflect our biggest hopes and dreams. I want to provide for my family, retire early, grow my wealth so I'll have more freedom, be known as a leader in my field. All of this can be worthwhile. But notice the theme: it's all about my personal aspirations and fulfillment. This is how most industrious Americans experience work—as a way to express my talents, accomplish my life goals, and feel significant. What if that's only part of the picture?

A bigger vision of work moves beyond the individual seeking personal fulfillment. What else does it include? Let's look at one man's famous encounter with Jesus that shook him free from his career-as-personal-fulfillment mind-set.

Zacchaeus was a tax collector who started listening to Jesus. His story is briefly told in Luke 19:1-10. The despised Roman government contracted collectors to enforce their tax edicts. In return, the collector got a cut from the booty. In fact, they were usually given liberal leeway in how much to charge. As long as Rome got her proper amount, the collector could keep whatever was above-and-beyond. So the job notoriously attracted the most cutthroat and driven.

Zacchaeus was chief tax collector in Jericho, a major import-export center just outside Jerusalem (19:1-2). As chief collector, he employed a cadre of subordinates and took a cut of their revenue. In other words, he sat atop a multi-level scheme in a tax-loaded city. Leaving no doubt, Luke tells us, "He was a chief tax collector and was rich" (19:2).

He publicly renounced underhanded profit: "Behold, Lord, the half of my goods I give to the poor. And if I have defrauded anyone of anything, I restore it fourfold" (19:8). So how did Zacchaeus' approach to work change? A quick reader would say, "He went from being dishonest to honest." While that's certainly true, his revolution went much deeper.

First, consider how Zacchaeus became a tax collector: he consciously chose personal wealth over community. Charging taxes for the Roman government while adding his own "convenience fee" meant making money by adding burden to his fellow citizens. Tax collectors were widely scorned, relegated to a shameful category with sinners. Zacchaeus surely knew this when he got into the business. But he decided it was better to make money than friends, better to be rich than a normal member of society. He valued his own personal advancement.

So his offer to give half his goods to the poor and repay anyone he had defrauded fourfold was more than a conversion to honesty. It was a decision to re-enter society and serve the common good. Zacchaeus suddenly saw his work and wealth as more than personal advancement! Now they were a way to serve his fellow man and reweave the social fabric.

This is work redeemed. It's not just about the money I make, the reputation I achieve, the freedom I enjoy. It's about a work-vision to bless others—my family, my city, my community, the needy—by serving the common good. Zacchaeus didn't just change from shady to honest.

HE GAVE UP WORKING TO ADVANCE HIMSELF IN ORDER TO WORK AS A BLESSING TO OTHERS.

✦✦✦ After encountering Jesus, Zacchaeus changed.

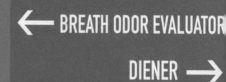
← BREATH ODOR EVALUATOR

DIENER →

WHAT THEY DO: ODOR JUDGES SMELL NASTY MORNING BREATH OR BREATH "INSULTED" WITH STRONG SCENTS, LIKE GARLIC OR COFFEE. THEY RATE THE BREATH ON A SCALE FROM ONE TO NINE, ONE BEING THE WORST, TO TEST ODOR-REDUCING PRODUCTS LIKE GUM OR MOUTHWASH, THEY SMELL THE BREATH AGAIN AND ASSIGN IT A NEW RATING.

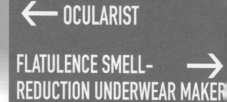
← OCULARIST

FLATULENCE SMELL- →
REDUCTION UNDERWEAR MAKER

WHAT THEY DO: IN SHORT, THEY PAINT ARTIFICIAL EYES. IT SOUNDS EASIER THAN IT IS, SINCE AS WITH REAL EYES, NO TWO ARE EXACTLY THE SAME.

← DOG SNIFFER

PAPER TOWEL SNIFFER →

WHAT THEY DO: ONCE A WEEK, THEY ANALYZE THE ODOR OF DOGS' BREATH TO TEST THE EFFECT OF THE ANIMALS' DIET ON THEIR TEETH. BREATH IS GRADED ON A SCALE OF 0 TO 10 AND IS CATEGORIZED AS SWEATY, SALTY, MUSTY, FUNGAL OR DECAYING.

← SAFECRACKER

PORTA-POTTY SERVICER →

WHAT THEY DO: WHEN COMBINATIONS ARE LOST OR FORGOTTEN, SAFECRACKERS USE THEIR EARS AND FINGERS TO OPEN THE SAFE.

ODD JOBS

WHAT THEY DO: PREPARE CADAVERS FOR THE PATHOLOGIST BEFORE AUTOPSIES ARE PERFORMED IN HOSPITALS.

...THEY ...CREATE UNDERWEAR ...PROTECTS AGAINST BAD HUMAN ...FOR PEOPLE WHO SUFFER FROM ...ROINTESTINAL PROBLEMS. THE ...RWEAR IS MADE WITH VARIOUS MATERIALS ...FILTERS TO HELP REMEDY HYDROGEN ...SULFIDE GASES, THE MAIN OFFENDER IN FOUL SMELLS.

WHAT THEY DO: PAPER TOWEL MANUFACTURERS PREFER THEIR PRODUCTS TO BE ODORLESS BEFORE, DURING AND AFTER THEIR USE. NATURALLY, PAPER TOWEL SNIFFERS ENSURE THAT ONCE A PAPER TOWEL IS USED, THERE IS NO NOTICEABLE SCENT.

...T THEY ...IKE REGULAR ...ROOMS, PORTABLE TOILETS ... MAINTENANCE, TOO. ONCE A WEEK, ...ICE WORKERS CLEAN THESE ...LE-STALL FACILITIES TO ACHIEVE ...AIN STANDARDS OF SANITATION.

RIBBON CANDY PULLER
What they do: After a heated combination of sugar, corn syrup, water and coloring agent has cooled, batches of different colors are laid out side by side. Someone then pulls the candy thin until it's about an inch wide. The final product is a multicolored hard candy.

BEER TESTER
What they do: Taste – and spit out – beer all day to approve new and existing flavors.

CRACK FILLER
What they do: Using a silicone sealant, they repair the wear and tear inflicted on monumental structures, like Mount Rushmore.

BALL TESTER
What they do: Assess basketballs, footballs, volleyballs and soccer balls for air-retention, inflation, roundness, weight and reboundability.

VIDEO GAME TESTER
What they do: For eight hours a day, five days a week, a group of males and females of all ages play video games. They repeat levels, games and characters, looking for any bugs and/or glitches in the software.

GOLD RECLAIMER
What they do: Scour old teeth for fillings, melt the gold from them with broken gold jewelry into tiny gold pellets, which are then resold to jewelers.

POTATO CHIP INSPECTOR
What they do: Search for overcooked or clumped chips to discard as they come down the assembly line.

WAX FIGURE MAKER
What they do: Mold wax to create figures, often for, but not limited to, the human form. Figures are often made in the likeness of people who have achieved historical or celebrity recognition.

FOLEY ARTIST
What they do: Use whatever they can find to create and record the noises used to make sound effects in films, like heavy footsteps, rolling thunder or creaking doors.

SESSION THREE | COURAGE

SCRIPTURE REFERENCES

Nehemiah 2:1–5 (ESV) "In the twentieth year of King Artaxerxes, when wine was before him, I took up the wine and gave it to the king. Now I had not been sad in his presence. And the king said to me, "Why is your face sad, seeing you are not sick? This is nothing but sadness of the heart." Then I was very much afraid. I said to the king, . . . "Why should not my face be sad, when the city, the place of my fathers' graves, lies in ruins, and its gates have been destroyed by fire?" Then the king said to me, "What are you requesting?" So I prayed to the God of heaven. And I said to the king, "If it pleases the king, and if your servant has found favor in your sight, . . . send me to Judah, to the city of my fathers' graves, that I may rebuild it."

Nehemiah 2:6–8 (ESV) And the king said to me . . . "How long will you be gone, and when will you return?" So it pleased the king to send me when I had given him a time. And I said to the king, "If it pleases the king, let letters be given me to the governors of the province Beyond the River, that they may let me pass through until I come to Judah, and a letter to Asaph, the keeper of the king's forest, that he may give me timber to make beams for the gates of the fortress of the temple, and for the wall of the city, and for the house that I shall occupy." And the king granted me what I asked."

Nehemiah 4:21–23 (ESV) "So we labored at the work, and half [of the men] held the spears from the break of dawn until the stars came out. I also said to the people at that time, 'Let every man and his servant pass the night within Jerusalem, that they may be a guard for us by night and may labor by day.' So neither I nor my brothers nor my servants nor the men of the guard who followed me, none of us took off our [work] clothes; [and] each kept his weapon at his right hand."

Nehemiah 12:27, 31, 43 (ESV) "And at the dedication of the wall of Jerusalem they sought the [priests] in all their places, to bring them to Jerusalem to celebrate the dedication with gladness, with thanksgivings and with singing . . . Then I brought the leaders of Judah up onto the wall and . . . [they] gave thanks. . . . And they offered great sacrifices that day and rejoiced, for God had made them rejoice with great joy."

1 Corinthians 11:1 (ESV) "Be imitators of me, as I am of Christ."

Ephesians 4:28 (ESV) "Let the thief no longer steal, but rather let him labor, doing honest work with his own hands, so that he may have something to share with anyone in need."

2 Thessalonians 3:10–12 (ESV) "If anyone is not willing to work, let him not eat. For we hear that some among you walk in idleness, not busy at work, but busybodies. Now such persons we command and encourage in the Lord Jesus Christ to do their work quietly and to earn their own living."

1 Timothy 5:8 (ESV) "If anyone does not provide for his relatives, and especially for members of his household, he has denied the faith and is worse than an unbeliever."

Essentials

Essentials Presented by Bryan Carter

I. INTRODUCTION

1. When a man embraces these ten essentials it will provide him with more opportunity, broader influence and greater success in his work.

II. TEN ESSENTIALS TO HELP YOU LIVE OUT THE BIBLICAL BLUEPRINT

1. Authentic Men are motivated by the ___GOSPEL___.

    •   Our primary motivation for wanting to excel at work should come from what Jesus has done for us and how He has transformed us and given us a new mindset.

    •   It is the gospel that ___Impowers___ us so that we can create and cultivate and be a life-giving presence in our work.

    •   "So brothers and sisters, since God has shown us great mercy, I beg you to offer your lives as a living sacrifice to him... Do not be shaped by this world; instead be changed within by a new way of thinking." Romans 12:1-2 (NCV)

    •   The gospel frees you to view your work as worshipping and serving God.

2. Do your ___BEST___ and over-deliver in your work.

    •   Many men settle for doing just "good enough" in their job.

    •   "In all the work you are doing, work the best you can. Work as if you were doing it for the Lord, not for people...You are serving the Lord Christ."
        Colossians 3:23-24 (NCV)

- "If a man is called to be a street sweeper, he should sweep streets like Michelangelo painted, or Beethoven composed music, or Shakespeare wrote poetry. He should sweep streets so well that all the hosts of heaven and earth will pause to say, 'Here lived a great street sweeper who did his job well.'"

  -Martin Luther King Jr.[1]

3. Become a master in your craft.

   - God authored every man's life and gifted each of us with _UNIQUE_ skills, talents and strengths.

   - "Do you see a man skillful in his work? He will stand before kings; he will not stand before obscure men." Proverbs 22:29 (ESV)

   - The skillful will be sought out for their expertise and will have great _INFLUENCE_ .

4. Work well with others.

   - An Authentic Man values "we" over _ME_ with his co-workers and employees. He has a heart of a servant-leader.

   - He is not _THREATENED_ by the successses or talents of others.

   - Authentic Men are also responsive to the leadership of those over them.

   - "Trustworthy messengers refresh like snow in summer. They revive the spirit of their employer." Proverbs 25:13 (NLT)

5. Don't be surprised by resistance.

   - _____ is a reality in our world.

[1] Martin Luther King, Jr, "The Three Dimensions of a Complete Life," in *A Knock at Midnight*, eds. Clayborne Carson and Peter Holloran (New York: Warner Books, 1998), 126.

- "I have said these things to you, that in me you may have peace...But take heart; I have overcome the world." John 16:33 (ESV)

- Authentic Men anticipate this resistance and put on their _____ face.

6. Bring integrity to the workplace.

- There are multiple opportunities daily to add to your reputation of integrity or to DESTROY it.

- "It takes a lifetime to build a reputation but you can lose it in a minute."
    - quote attributed to Will Rogers

- "Whoever walks in integrity walks securely, but he who makes his ways crooked will be found out." Proverbs 10:9 (ESV)

7. Healthy ambition can be a good thing.

- Every man's heart can be tempted toward a deep, dark PRIDE and narcissism.

- Another extreme to avoid is killing ambition and resting in mediocrity.

- A godly, REDEEMED ambition should be our goal.

- "Whatever you do, do it all for the glory of God." 1 Corinthians 10:31

8. Go find the information you need to excel in the workplace.

- Authentic Men GO GET the help they need to grow in their work.

9. Pursue a job that you can enjoy, are good at and that will adequately provide.

- It takes ___COURAGE___ to pursue change and transition.

- Authentic Men look for the right job fit.

10. Rest and celebrate.

- "Human beings are not designed to run like computers, at high speeds, continuously, for long periods of time. When we try to mimic the machines we're meant to run, they end up running us. In fact, we're designed to pulse. Our most basic survival need is to spend and renew energy. We're hardwired to make waves - to be alert during the day and to sleep at night, but also to work at high intensity for limited periods of time and then rest and refuel. Instead, [most of us] lead increasingly linear lives, forever spending down our energy without fully or effectively renewing it."[2] -Tony Schwartz

- An Authentic Man works hard but knows when to turn work ___OFF___.

See Summary of the 10 Essentials on pages 64-65.

[2] Tony Schwartz, *The Way We're Working Isn't Working*, (New York: Free Press, 2010).

DISCUSSION / REFLECTION QUESTIONS

1. Which of the ten essentials is easiest for you to embrace? Which is the most difficult?

HARD WORK   ACCEPT PEOPLE WHO DON'T WANT
LEARN   TO WORK

2. How does the gospel, what Jesus has already done for you, affect your view of work and motivate you excel in your career?

UNDERSTANDING THAT ALL THE SKILLS,
JOB OPPORTUNITIES, AND CERTAIN PEOPLE IN MY LIFE,
CREATED EVERYTHING I HAVE

3. Essential number six was "Authentic Men bring integrity to the workplace." For your particular line of work, what are the typical ways a man's integrity can be challenged or tested?

POLITICAL: ASKING TO TAKE A PATH THAT GOES AGAINST
WHAT I BELIEVE GOD WOULD WANT.

4. Have you accepted the primary responsibility for your own vocational growth and development? Can y identify the resources or people that could help you grow vocationally? Why is this important?

I ALWAYS RECOGNIZED THE PEOPLE I KNEW WHO
COULD HELP ME LEARN.

5. For essential number nine, "pursue a good job fit," Bryan said that we should pursue a job we enjoy, a good at, and can make enough money doing. Have you found that balance in your job? Explain.

RESOURCES ON THE FOLLOWING PAGES:

- The 10 Essentials (p. 64-65)

- Resistance is a Reality (p. 66-69)

- THE RED ZONE: Gospel Identity (70-71)

ten essentials

Our primary motivation for "excelling" at work comes from the gospel.

The gospel changes everything. Our motivation comes from what Jesus has done for us and how He transformed us.

Do your best & over-deliver in your work.

Seeing your work primarily as a service to the Lord is a game-changer. It unleashes you to bring a mind-set of excellence to your work.

Master your craft.

Discover your strengths, understand your talents, and develop your skills. Those who become exceptionally skillful in what they do, will more than likely expand their influence.

Work well with others.

An Authentic Man values "we" over "me." Being a positive team player goes a long way to being a life-giving presence.

Expect resistance... push through, work hard, and trust God.

Resistance will be a reality in this broken world. Anticipate this resistance and put on the warrior face, man up, and press through.

1   2   3   4   5

TO LIVING OUT
A BIBLICAL VIEW OF WORK

Bring integrity to the workplace.

The peace and security that come from walking with integrity is life-giving to your soul and is essential to living out God's vision for your work.

Healthy ambition can be a good thing.

Redeemed ambition seeks greatness in life as a means to an end—to bless others and bring glory to God as He made us in His image.

Go find the information you need to excel in the workplace.

Authentic Men accept the responsibility for being prepared, and hunger for growth in every area of their life. Get the help you need to grow in your work. No one else is going to do that for you.

If possible, pursue a job that you can enjoy, are good at, and can make money doing.

Look for the right job fit where you can come alive and bring life to others. Be willing to make the courageous adjustments to find it.

Rest and celebrate.

An Authentic Man works hard, but he knows when to turn work off. He balances the tension between work and rest.

6   7   8   9   10

RESISTANCE
IS A REALITY

Ever feel like there are forces working against you in your work? This **HUMOROUS** story of a hard-working bricklayer filling out his "accident report form" reminds us to never be surprised by a little resistance in our work-lives.

DEAR SIR,

I am writing in response to your request for additional information in Block #3 of the accident reporting form. I put 'Poor Planning' as the cause of my accident. You asked for a fuller explanation and I trust the following details will be sufficient.

I am a bricklayer by trade. On the day of the accident, I was working alone on the roof of a new six-story building. When I completed my work, I found I had some bricks left over which, when weighed later, were found to weigh 240 pounds. Rather than carry the bricks down by hand, I decided to lower them in a barrel by using a pulley which was attached to the side of the building at the sixth floor.

Securing the rope at ground level, I went up to the roof, swung the barrel out and loaded the bricks into it. Then I went down and untied the rope, holding it tightly to insure a slow descent of the 240 pounds of bricks. You will note on the accident reporting form that my weight is 135 pounds. Due to my surprise at being jerked off the ground so suddenly, I lost my presence of mind and forgot to let go of the rope. Needless to say, I proceeded at a rapid rate up the side of the building.

In the vicinity of the third floor, I met the barrel which was now proceeding downward at an equally impressive speed. This explains the fractured skull, minor abrasions, and the broken collarbone, as listed in Section 3, accident reporting form.

Slowed only slightly, I continued my rapid ascent, not stopping until the fingers of my right hand were two knuckles deep into the pulley which I mentioned in Paragraph 2 of this correspondence. Fortunately, by this time I had regained my presence of mind and was able to hold tightly to the rope, in spite of the excruciating pain I was now beginning to experience.

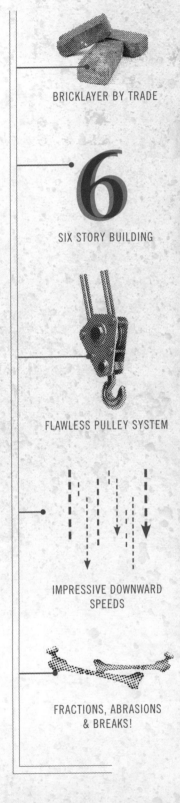

BRICKLAYER BY TRADE

6

SIX STORY BUILDING

FLAWLESS PULLEY SYSTEM

IMPRESSIVE DOWNWARD SPEEDS

FRACTIONS, ABRASIONS & BREAKS!

At approximately the same time, however, the barrel of bricks hit the ground and the bottom broke out of the barrel.

Now devoid of the weight of the bricks, the barrel weighed approximately 50 pounds. I refer you again to my weight. As you might imagine, I began a rapid descent down the side of the building. In the vicinity of the third floor, I met the barrel coming up. This accounts for the two fractured ankles, broken tooth, and severe lacerations of my legs and lower body.

Here my luck began to change slightly. The encounter with the barrel seemed to slow me enough to lessen my injuries when I fell into the pile of bricks and fortunately only three vertebrae were cracked. I am sorry to report, however, as I lay there on the pile of bricks, in pain, unable to move and watching the empty barrel six stories above me, I again lost my composure and presence of mind and let go of the rope.

The empty 50-pound barrel, weighing more than the rope I had let go, fell rapidly to earth, resulting in the two broken forearms and wrists when I raised by arms to protect myself.

I hope this information satisfactorily fulfills your request for further information.

For more about this popular urban legend, check out MythBusters miniMyth episode at *http://www.youtube.com/watch?v=Vt230Pd1oSo.*

HIGH-FLYING, RECKLESS BARREL

135

* WEIGHT REMINDER*

BOTTOM OF THE SIX-STORY BUILDING

GOSPEL IDENTITY

Every Good Endeavor, p. 73, by Tim Keller

"Many **modern people** seek a kind of salvation... self-esteem & self-worth...

from **CAREER SUCCESS**. This leads us to seek only high-paying, high-status jobs, and to "worship" them in perverse ways.

But the GOSPEL *[the good news of Jesus]* frees us from the relentless pressure of having to **PROVE OURSELVES** & **SECURE OUR IDENTITY** through work, for we are already PROVEN and SECURE.

All work now becomes a way to love the God who saved us freely; and by extension,

A way to LOVE OUR NEIGHBOR."

SCRIPTURE REFERENCES

Proverbs 10:9 (ESV) "Whoever walks in integrity walks securely, but he who makes his ways crooked will be found out."

Proverbs 22:29 (ESV) "Do you see a man skillful in his work? He will stand before kings; he will not stand before obscure men."

Proverbs 25:13 (NLT) "Trustworthy messengers refresh like snow in summer. They revive the spirit of their employer."

Romans 12:1–2 (NCV) "So brothers and sisters, since God has shown us great mercy, I beg you to offer your lives as a living sacrifice to him. . . . Do not be shaped by this world; instead be changed within by a new way of thinking."

1 Corinthians 10:31 (ESV) "Whatever you do, do all to the glory of God."

Colossians 3:23-24 (NCV) "In all the work you are doing, work the best you can. Work as if you were doing it for the Lord, not for people. . . .You are serving the Lord Christ."

SUPPORTING RESOURCES

Timothy Keller with Katherine Leary Alsdorf. *Every Good Endeavor: Connecting Your Work to God's Work.* Dutton, 2012. Tim Keller shows how the gospel is relevant for our everyday lives, including our work life. This is an outstanding resource for understanding God's purposes for work.

Dave Harvey. *Rescuing Ambition.* Crossway, 2010. Dave Harvey argues that the concept of "ambition" has often gotten a bad reputation. Harvey maintains that, when put to work for the glory of God, ambition can be quite useful and pious.

* The content in the resources above does not necessarily reflect the opinion of Authentic Manhood. Readers should utilize these resources but form their own opinions.

SESSION 5

Traps

SESSION **FIVE** | Training Guide

Traps Presented by Tierce Green

I. INTRODUCTION

1. These work traps can rob us of our joy, our influence, and our integrity.

II. SIX TRAPS TO AVOID AT WORK

1. The _UNREALISTIC_ Expectations Trap

   - When our work doesn't meet our expectations, we can easily give in to _DISAPPOINTMENT_, bitterness, and cynicism.

   - Genesis 3:17-18 teaches us that, as a result of Adam's sin, work will now involve "painful toil" and be frustrated by "thorns and thistles."

   - "All work and human effort [are] marked by frustration and lack of fulfillment... Work is not itself a curse, but it now lies with all other aspects of human life under the curse of sin."[1] - Tim Keller

   - Authentic Men manage tension between a _BIBLICAL_ vision of work and the realities of a broken world.

2. The Significance Trap

   - Performance and success have become the _MAIN SOURCE_ of his significance.

   "We are the first culture in history where men define themselves solely by performing and achieving in the workplace. It is the way you become somebody and feel good about your life... There has never been more psychological, social, and emotional pressure in the marketplace than there is at this very moment."[2]
   - Tim Keller

   - Only Jesus is a sure _FOUNDATION_ for your significance and identity.

[1] Tim Keller, *Every Good Endeavor*, (New York: Dutton, 2012), 89-90.
[2] Richard E. Simmons III, *The True Measure of a Man*, (Mobile, AL: Evergreen Press, 2011), 25.

3. The Money Trap

    •   Materialism - when a man defines himself, not by his production, but by his consumption.

        ◦   Materialism won't ___SATISFY___ .

        ◦   "He who loves money will not be satisfied with money, nor he who loves wealth with his income." Ecclesiastes 5:10 (ESV)

        ◦   God calls us to give and bless others, not just consume.

    •   Inappropriate debt - when a man unnecessarily or unwisely ___BORROWS___ money he doesn't have.

        ◦   The Bible reminds us that, "The borrower is the slave of the lender." Proverbs 22:7 (ESV)

        ◦   Debt should always be approached with wisdom and some trepidation.

    •   The Fear of Money - when a man thinks that money, in and of itself, is a ___BAD___ thing.

        ◦   The Bible says that the " ___LOVE___ of money" is evil.

        ◦   Use your skill to generate money so you can give life to others.

        ◦   Be certain your ultimate ___HOPE___ and happiness is in the life-giving grace of Jesus and not the size of your bank account.

4. The Compartment Trap

    •   This is when a man compartmentalizes the different parts of his life.

        ◦   According to *Psychology Today*, "Men have an uncanny and dangerous ability to compartmentalize their lives into mutually exclusive rooms whose walls have no windows or doors."[3]

³ Jay Kent-Ferraro, "Surprised by Love: Betrayal: What's Wrong With Men?," *Psychology Today*, June 9, 2011, http://www.psychologytoday.com/blog/surprised-love/201106/betrayal-whats-wrong-men.

- Authentic Men integrate their __FAITH__ into their work lives.

5. The Sex Trap

- The sex trap is when a man allows __LUST__ to invade his work-life.

- Authentic Men proactively create an environment where women can feel safe and comfortable, where they are respected, and where they are valued. 70%

- Having a __DOUBLE__ life will eventually tear your soul apart.

- Don't try to fight this battle by yourself.

- Follow the advice of 1 Corinthians 6:18 (ESV), which tells us to "flee from sexual immorality."

6. The Retirement Trap

- Around 1900, 75% of men over the age of 65 were still working. In fact, most men worked as long as they were able and if a man wasn't working, it was most often because he was disabled.[4]

- In many modern cultures, retirement has become the ultimate __GOAL__ in a man's work life.

- The Bible doesn't make retirement the ultimate goal of life.

- Work, in some form or fashion, should be a part of every __SEASON__ of every man's life.

- Full retirement is going to be unattainable for most of us:

  ° 75% of Americans nearing retirement in 2010 had less than $30,000 in their retirement accounts.[5]

 [4] Georgetown University Law Center, "A Timeline of the Evolution of Retirement in the United States," (Washington, D.C., 2010), http://scholarship.law.georgetown.edu/cgi/viewcontent.cgi?article=1049&context=legal.
[5] Teresa Ghilarducci, "Our Ridiculous Approach to Retirement," The New York Times, July 21, 2012, http://www.nytimes.com/2012/07/22/opinion/sunday/our-ridic...

- UCLA's legendary basketball coach, John Wooden, is an excellent example of how to handle retirement:

  "After winning his tenth NCAA basketball title at age sixty-five, [Wooden] retired from coaching but [he] remained involved at UCLA, wrote a number of books and was often quoted and consulted."[6]

Wise is the man who takes note of these traps and not only avoids them, but replaces them with a Biblical vision for work.

7. THE I DESERVE TRAP:

[6] Hugh Whelchel, "How Should Christians Think About Retirement?," *Institute for Faith, Work & Economics*, August 15, 2013, http://blog.tifwe.org/how-should-christians-think-about-retirement/

SESSION FIVE | TRAPS

DISCUSSION/ REFLECTION QUESTIONS

1. Read the quote below and discuss its relevance for how men think about their work. Why do you think our culture puts so much emphasis on work?

"We are the first culture in history where men define themselves solely by performing and achieving in the workplace. It is the way you become somebody and feel good about your life . . . there has never been more psychological, social, and emotional pressure in the marketplace than there is at this very moment."[7]

2. Tierce talked about three different strains of the money trap: materialism, inappropriate debt, and the fear of money. Which of those did you identify with the most?

FEAR OF MONEY

3. Do you struggle with the compartment trap? Are you the same person at work as you are at home? Discuss.

4. How have you traditionally thought of retirement? Did this session impact your view?

[7] Richard E. Simmons III, *The True Measure of a Man*, (Mobile, AL: Evergreen Press, 2011), 25.

RESOURCES ON THE FOLLOWING PAGES:

- Money and Financial Health (p. 80-83)

- Rethinking Retirement (p. 84-87)

- THE RED ZONE: Statistics from the Workplace (p. 88-89)

104

MONEY

&

FINANCIAL HEALTH

BY MIKE BOSCHETTI

· ·

MONEY. IT'S FRONT AND CENTER IN THIS WORLD EVERY DAY. IT'S A BIG DEAL. As a man, how should we think about it? If a man spends less than he earns and invests the difference over a long period of time, he most probably will accumulate a significant amount of wealth by the end of his days.

HOWEVER, IS THAT THE RIGHT GOAL?

As we heard in this session, Solomon said in Ecclesiastes 5:10, "*He who loves money will not be satisfied with money, nor he who loves wealth with his income.*" However, the idea of being wealthy and all that entails seems to be the goal of most men and, as a result, men fall into three common money traps. **Let's address each one and establish some strategies to combat them.**

FEAR OF MONEY

. . . .

IF YOU HAVE A FEAR OF MONEY, (FEAR YOU WON'T HAVE ENOUGH, FEAR YOU WILL BE POSSESSED BY IT, ETC.), BEGIN TO BE GENEROUS in sharing with others. Not only will the fear subside, but you will be blessed more than you could ever imagine.

One of the tenets of being an Authentic Man is to be a life-giving spirit. The idea of earning money so we can use it to help bless others is very compelling. Jesus' quote, *"It is more blessed to give than to receive,"* has been proven in the lives of many through the ages. I have seen that same principle played out in my own life as well as in the lives of scores of individuals and couples I have counseled through the years. Even the geography of the nation of Israel testifies to this:

There are two primary bodies of water in Israel. At the Sea of Galilee, there is fishing, boating, picnicking by the shore, etc. It is beautiful and full of life. However, at the Dead Sea, there is no fishing, no boating and no picnicking by its shores, for it has no life and its water feels like oil. An interesting fact is that both bodies of water are fed by the same source. Why is one alive and the other dead? The answer is one "gives" and the other does not. The Sea of Galilee is "alive". It is fed by the water table in northern Israel, and has an outlet that "gives" to the Jordan River. The Jordan River runs south and feeds the Dead Sea. However, the Dead Sea is as its name states—dead. The difference is that the Dead Sea has no outlet; it doesn't "give" its water to anything. It keeps it all, since it is the lowest place on earth.

Want to overcome your fear of money? Give generously to others.

UNWISE DEBT

. . . .

IN TODAY'S WESTERN CULTURE, a family of four has an average of $26,000 in consumer debt. When college debt is added, the total is $42,000.

Though Scripture doesn't prohibit acquiring debt, it clearly warns about the hazards of being in debt, *"The borrower is the slave of the lender,"* Proverbs 22:7. Anyone who has ever been in significant debt knows the truth of that statement. Money you would like to use for something else has to be paid to the lender every month (for what seems like forever).

So what can be done?

If already in debt, simply decide to quit going further into debt— cut up the credit cards and start living on a budget which includes repaying debt more rapidly than paying the "minimum payment." Sure, there could be some pain involved; if you have been living above the standard of living your income would indicate while you were incurring debt, you most likely will have to live below that standard of living during debt repayment. That is what an Authentic Man does—rejects passivity, accepts responsibility and courageously faces difficult choices, doing the right thing.

If you are considering borrowing money, I recommend that you have at least two methods to repay—one would be from income and the other would be from the asset you are borrowing against. That implies strongly that borrowing money for perishables (where most credit card debt is incurred) is never a good idea, because there is only one source for repayment; if emergencies

104

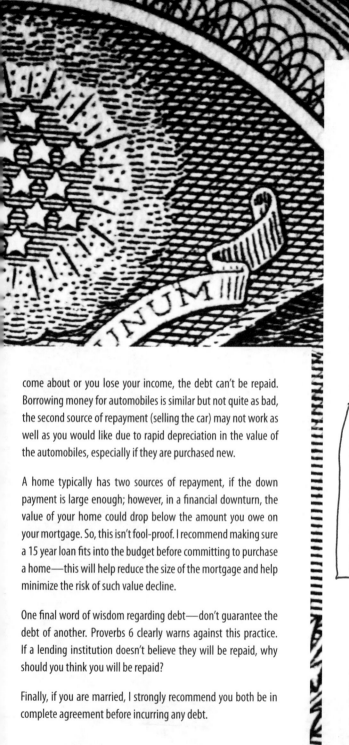

come about or you lose your income, the debt can't be repaid. Borrowing money for automobiles is similar but not quite as bad, the second source of repayment (selling the car) may not work as well as you would like due to rapid depreciation in the value of the automobiles, especially if they are purchased new.

A home typically has two sources of repayment, if the down payment is large enough; however, in a financial downturn, the value of your home could drop below the amount you owe on your mortgage. So, this isn't fool-proof. I recommend making sure a 15 year loan fits into the budget before committing to purchase a home—this will help reduce the size of the mortgage and help minimize the risk of such value decline.

One final word of wisdom regarding debt—don't guarantee the debt of another. Proverbs 6 clearly warns against this practice. If a lending institution doesn't believe they will be repaid, why should you think you will be repaid?

Finally, if you are married, I strongly recommend you both be in complete agreement before incurring any debt.

MATERIALISM

· ·

THIS MONEY TRAP CAN BE ADDRESSED by considering the message in 1 Chronicles 29:11-12 (as well as numerous other Scriptures). God owns everything—He owns it and we manage it—we are His stewards.

The business world uses the term fiduciary in a similar manner; an example would be the trust department of a bank. Fiduciaries manage other peoples' money and can't spend the money for anything other than what the trust instrument dictates.

Luke 16:11-12 says *"Therefore if you have not been faithful in the use of unrighteous wealth, who will entrust the true riches to you? And if you have not been faithful in the use of that which is another's, who will give you that which is your own?"* (NASB).

If Authentic Men managed the Owner's money according to the "trust agreement" (Scripture), I wonder if the pursuit of materialism would be an issue? Matthew 6:33 says, *"Seek first the kingdom of God and his righteousness, and all these things [life provisions] will be added to you"* (ESV).

SUMMARY

· ·

ALL TRAPS ARE BEST NEGOTIATED WHEN you know they are present and you have a strategy to address them. Money traps are no different. After this session, we should all recognize that they are present. Adopting the strategies noted above should provide a way to navigate the traps in a way that will help you be an Authentic Man in this crucial area.

by Tierce Green

RETHINKING
RETIREMENT

Tierce Green is a man who understands the importance of being positioned well through each season of life. Still wielding a sword in his fifties, he recently stepped into a new challenge as *Pastor of House Churches* at Church Project in The Woodlands, Texas.

HE WAS BORN NATHAN BIRNBAUM,

an actor, comedian and writer who actively worked at his craft all his life and became a prominent part of American cultural history in the 20th Century. His arched eyebrow and dry humor punctuated by cigar smoke became his iconic trademark. We knew him as George Burns and he lived—really lived—to be a hundred.

His faith was a little sketchy. In his own words, "I was Jewish, but I was out of practice."[1] Nevertheless, his perspective of work, retirement and aging gets at the heart of the Authentic Man's view of work. He said, "Age to me means nothing. I can't get old; I'm working. I was old when I was 21 and out of work."[2]

Retirement can rob us of our joy and influence.

Most people don't see it as a trap unless you're talking about not being able to retire. But, the notion of retirement is not found in the Bible. It is actually a Western 20th Century invention. According to a study conducted at GEORGETOWN UNIVERSITY, around the year 1900, 75% of men over the age of 65 were still working. Most men worked as long as they were able, and if a man wasn't working it was most often because he was disabled.[3]

In stark contrast was a speech given by William Osler in 1905 at Johns Hopkins University School of Medicine. Osler was one of the most illustrious physicians in our history. His claim to fame outside the medical profession was through what became known as *The Fixed Period* controversy about the usefulness of old men. In his valedictory address, Osler remarked that men older than 60 should be retired. Osler said it was a matter of fact that age 25 to 40 in a worker's career was "the constructive period." He believed that workers between ages 40 and 60 were uncreative, and therefore, merely tolerable. He hated to say it, because he was nearing the cut-off himself, but after age 60 he believed the average worker was useless and should be put out to pasture. He attempted a joking referral to Anthony Trollope's novel *The Fixed Period*, which suggested that men older than that be chloroformed.[4]

Osler's provocative speech generated much debate and controversy. It was a ridiculous idea, but here we are a hundred years later, and many of us are relinquishing what could be our most productive years of influence. A lot of guys think that life begins at retirement—the ultimate end zone where a man is granted permission to live a self-absorbed existence for the final chapter of his life.

Aiming at a target where we will one day have enough wealth to retire comfortably, free from responsibility, is one of life's biggest mistakes. We may hit the bull's eye only to discover that we chose the wrong target. Oftentimes, retirement doesn't feel like a reward for a lifetime of hard work; it feels more like a punishment. Ernest Hemingway said, "Retirement is the ugliest word in the language." If you retire from something with nothing to retire to, life feels empty and hollow.

Men in pursuit of Authentic Manhood know that the typical view of retirement is contrary to the truth of God's Word. You may retire from having to draw the same paycheck, but you never retire from giving your life away and making strategic investments in others.

Here are 5 things you can start doing right now to avoid the Retirement Trap:

1 | ADOPT A HIGHER MOTIVATION FOR WORK

Consider these four motivations:[5]

→ **PAYCHECK DRIVEN** | Working because you have to.

→ **PASSION DRIVEN** | Leveraging work to do something meaningful and make a difference.

→ **PHILANTHROPY DRIVEN** | Seeing work as a platform to help others, allowing you to make money and give things away.

→ **PURPOSE DRIVEN** | Strategically positioning yourself throughout your career to make an eternal difference.

Working because you have to is an honorable reality of life, but for work to be truly satisfying you need a higher motivation. A higher motivation for work will drive you to develop a plan to pay off all your debts, even your mortgage. You will make wise financial moves now so you can be more agile and mobile in the winter season of your life. Invest eternally starting now.

2 | STAY ACTIVE & PRODUCTIVE.

Steve Jobs was a master at unveiling Apple's new technology in his keynote addresses. Just when you thought everything had been revealed, Jobs would electrify the crowd by saying, "but there is one more thing... " Jobs lost his battle with cancer at age 56, which many considered to be the prime of his life because he was always in active pursuit of "one more thing." Others at 56 are way past their prime because they stopped learning, stopped producing, conditioned for retirement.

We have a divine partnership with God creating and cultivating. Psalm 92:12-14 (NIV) says, "The righteous will flourish like a palm tree, they will grow like a cedar of Lebanon; planted in the house of the LORD, they will flourish in the courts of our God. They will still bear fruit in old age, they will stay fresh and green ... "

1. George Burns, *Gracie: A Love Story*, (New York: G. P. Putnam's Sons, 1988), 64.

2. Albin Krebs and Robert McG. Thomas, "Notes on People; George Burns, 85, on the Secret of Staying Young," *The New York Times*, January 21, 1988, *http://www.nytimes.com/1981/01/21/nyregion/notes-on-people-george-burns-85-on-the-secret-of-staying-young.html*.

3. Georgetown University Law Center, "A Timeline of the Evolution of Retirement in the United States," (Washington, D.C., 2010), *http://scholarship.law.georgetown.edu/cgi/viewcontent.cgi?article=1049&context=legal*.

4. Laura Davidow Hirshbein, "William Osler and *The Fixed Period*: Conflicting Medical and Popular Ideas About Old Age," *Arch Intern Med* 161, no. 17 *http//archinte.jamanetwork.com/article.aspx?articleid=648994&resultClick=3.*

5. *Men's Fraternity Classic: Winning at Work and Home* by Dr. Robert Lewis. ©2011 Authentic Manhood

6. *33 The Series, Volume 1: A Man and His Design, Session 6: Seasons* ©2012 Authentic Manhood

3 NEVER LAY DOWN YOUR SWORD.

Joshua lived to be 110 and led the conquest of Canaan during the last thirty years of his life. Caleb was in his eighties when he asked for the hill country of Hebron—not to retire in a quiet little cabin and enjoy the sunset of his life. He knew there were giants in them thar hills! He was still wielding a sword at age 85! (Joshua 14:6-15)

4 BE STRATEGICALLY POSITIONED THROUGH EACH SEASON OF LIFE.

Transitioning well through the seasons of a man's life is critical for maximum impact and lasting fulfillment.[6] If you find yourself in an environment that devalues the wisdom and experience of older men, an organization that thinks investing in the next generation means clearing the landscape of leaders over forty, start developing an exit strategy now. It's unhealthy, unbiblical, and a serious indicator of nearsightedness. On the other hand, don't be the old guy who is out of touch and doesn't know how to grow and adapt. Restrain from pushing your personal preferences. Learn instead to share your wisdom and experience about proven principles that are timeless and effective.

5 LOCK ARMS WITH MEN WHO ARE LIVING A LIFE OF TRUTH, PASSION & PURPOSE.

Proverbs 13:20 (NIV) says, "Walk with the wise and become wise, for a companion of fools suffers harm." That is a lifelong principle for success through each season of life. Surround yourself with self-absorbed men who primarily define themselves by titles, salaries, and 401ks, and you will begin to measure yourself by the same values. Lock arms with men who practice the truth of God's Word—men who are in active pursuit of a life filled with truth, passion and purpose—and you will experience a full life for all of your life.

55%. SAID THAT BEING PAID COMPETITIVELY WITHIN THE LOCAL MARKET IS IMPORTANT

60%. OF AMERICAN WORKERS SAID THAT COMPENSATION WAS VERY IMPORTANT

http://www.shrm.org/LegalIssues/StateandLocalResources/StateandLocalStatutesandRegulations/Documents/12-0537%202012_JobSatisfaction_FNL_online.pdf

http://www.shrm.org/LegalIssues/StateandLocalResources/StateandLocalStatutesandRegulations/Documents/12-0537%202012_JobSatisfaction_FNL_online.pdf

43%.

OF MEN FEEL UNDERPAID

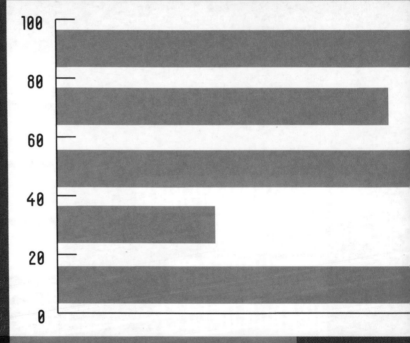

http://jobs.aol.com/articles/2013/03/06/americans-stressed-underpaid-overworked-survey/

39%. OF PEOPLE PLACED MOST IMPORTANCE ON THE MEANINGFULNESS OF THE JOB

20%. OF MEN ADMIT TO WATCHING PORNOGRAPHY AT WORK

http://www.shrm.org/LegalIssues/StateandLocalResources/StateandLocalStatutesandRegulations/Documents/12-0537%20201

65% OF PEOPLE ARE GLOBALLY UNSATISFIED WITH THEIR JOB AND WANT NEW WORK

http://www.forbes.com/sites/susanadams/2012/05/18/new-survey-majority-of-employees-dissatisfied/

70% OF AMERICAN WORKERS EXPERIENCE STRESS-RELATED ILLNESS

Dan Miller, 48 Days To the Work You Love

STATISTICS
FROM THE
WORKPLACE

the RED ZONE

17.6% OF PEOPLE FEEL UNDEREMPLOYED

87% SAID THEY FEEL OVERWORKED. OF THAT GROUP, 38% SAID THEY WERE SATISFIED WITH THEIR WORK-LIFE BALANCE

http://www.forbes.com/sites/susanadams/2012/12/11/new-survey-were-almost-all-overworked-but-we-dont-really-mind/

SCRIPTURE REFERENCES

Proverbs 22:7 (ESV) "... The borrower is the slave of the lender."

Ecclesiastes 5:10 (ESV) "He who loves money will not be satisfied with money, nor he who loves wealth with his income."

1 Corinthians 6:18 (ESV) "Flee from sexual immorality."

SUPPORTING RESOURCES

Timothy Keller with Katherine Leary Alsdorf. *Every Good Endeavor: Connecting Your Work to God's Work.* Dutton, 2012. In part two of this work, Keller and Alsdorf discuss the traps of work: how work can become fruitless, pointless, selfish, or an idol.

Richard E. Simmons. *The True Measure of a Man: How Perceptions of Success, Achievement, and Recognition Fail Men in Difficult Times.* Evergreen, 2010. This book is a must read for all men. It helps men fight the significance trap, the most pervasive work trap among men.

Catalyzers

SESSION SIX | Training Guide

Catalyzers Presented by John Bryson

I. INTRODUCTION

1. Work-Catalyzers: To catalyze means to accelerate ... to expand ... to inspire.

II. SIX WORK CATALYZERS

1. Pursue Self-Awareness

- As Authentic Men, we need to know who we are, and who we are ___NOT___.

- According to Gallup, only one-third of workers get to utilize their main strengths every day in their work.[1]

- "Most people think they know what they are ___GOOD___ at, they are usually wrong."[2] - Peter Drucker

- God has given each one of us unique gifts and we are to use that gifting to serve one another. (1 Peter 4:10, 11)

- Here are two ways you can pursue self-awareness and discover your strengths:

  ° Invest in some personality and assessment inventories.

  ° Find wise and objective counselors or ___COACHES___ who can give you honest feedback.

    - "... In an abundance of counselors there is safety." Proverbs 11:14 (ESV)

- A strength is not just something that you are good at, it's also something that leaves you ___ENERGGES___ and feeling strong.

- If you're not working from your strengths, you are six times less likely to be engaged in your job.

[1] Tom Rath, *StrengthsFinder 2.0*, (New York: Gallup, 2007), ii.
[2] Ibid., 15.

2. Play _OFFENSE_

   • Remember our manhood definition:

     -Reject Passivity
     -Accept Responsibility
     -Lead Courageously
     -Invest Eternally

   • Too many men just settle and remain _STUCK_.

   • Move toward the right fit trusting that God will direct your steps.

3. Establish A Track Record Of _FAITHFULNESS_

   • "Whatever you do, work heartily, as for the Lord and not for men, knowing that from the Lord you will receive the inheritance as your reward. You are serving the Lord Christ." - Colossians 3:23-24 (ESV)

   • A faithful worker is certainly better positioned to be a _LIFE-GIVING_ presence.

   • The _GOSPEL_ inspires and motivates us to be faithful in all that God has called us to do, including our work.

4. Find the Right Work Teammates

   • Almost every leader in the Bible that God worked through to do great things and had major influence had a great team around them.

   • Jesus modeled this by being part of a great team with His disciples.

   • _PAUL_ partnered with teammates to plant churches and carry out his mission.

- King David surrounded himself with a valued and a trusted team of men.

- As much as it is possible for you, fight to have the best possible team of people around you.

5. Establish a Culture of Encouragement

   - The Bible places a premium on encouragement:

     ○ "Encourage one another and build one another up." 1 Thessalonions 5:11 (ESV)

     ○ "Look not only to [your] own interests, but also to the interests of others." Philippians 2:4 (ESV)

     ○ "Be devoted to one another with mutual love, showing eagerness in honoring one another." Romans 12:10 (NET)

   - One of the best things you can do is create an encouraging work culture - an environment where employees are energized and motivated, appreciated and supported.

   - Create and cultivate a work environment that is ___LIFE-GIVING___ to your employees or coworkers.

6. Use your Work-Related Talents to Bless Your Community

   - Lay your ___SKILL-SET___ over the deepest needs of the city and figure out how you can help it and help others flourish.

   - God intended your work to be a means to give life to others.

     ○ "When the righteous do well the city rejoices... a city is exalted by the blessing provided from the upright." Proverbs 11:10-11 (NET)

° "Seek the welfare of the city where I have sent you into exile, and pray to the LORD on its behalf, for in its welfare you will find your welfare." Jeremiah 29:7 (ESV)

- Authentic Men see their work as a __CALLING__ from God.

III. CONCLUSION

1. Remember our Biblical Blueprint for Work:

   - What **is** work? It's a vocation - God's personal and purposeful call on your life.

   - What are we to **do** in our work? Like God did in the garden, we are to create and cultivate.

   - Who are we to **be** in our work? Like Jesus, we are to be a "life-giving presence."

   See Biblical Blueprint on pages 34-35

2. Remember that our manhood definition reminds us to play offense:

   - Play offense by rejecting a passive "I'm stuck" work mindset.

   - Play offense by accepting the responsibility to live-out the work Blueprint we've given you.

   - Play offense by leading other men through a deliberate process to understand God's design for work.

   - Play offense by seeing your work as a way to invest eternally and be a difference-maker in the world

3. Remember the apostle Paul's closing words in one of his letters to the Corinthians:

   - "Beloved brothers, be steadfast, immovable, always abounding in the work of the Lord, knowing that in the Lord your labor is not in vain." 1 Corinthians 15:58 (ESV)

DISCUSSION/ REFLECTION QUESTIONS

1. Can you name your strengths—things you're both good at and that leave you feeling strong? What are they?

2. Are you "playing offense" right now in your work-life? Or, are you struggling with an "I'm stuck" mentality? What's the next strategic move you need to make at your job or in your career?

3. What are some strategic ways you can use your work-related talents to be a life-giving presence and bless your community?

4. Remember from 33, Volume One, "A Man and His Design," our manhood definition is to "reject passivity, accept responsibility, lead courageously, and invest eternally." What would it look like to apply this definition to your work life?

COURAGES LEADERSHIP INSPIRES OTHERS TO EXCEL

RESOURCES ON THE FOLLOWING PAGES:

- The Truth Behind the Catalyzers (p. 98-99)

- Bless Your Community (p. 100-101)

- THE RED ZONE: Well Said (p. 102-103)

- Additional Resources (p. 104-105)

- Action Plan (p. 107)

THE TRUTH BEHIND THE CATALYZERS

Pursue Self-Awareness

"As each has received a gift, use it to serve one another, as good stewards of God's varied grace." **1 PETER 4 :10 (ESV)**

"Where there is no guidance, a people falls, but in an abundance of counselors there is safety." **PROVERBS 11:14 (ESV)**

"In his grace, God has given us different gifts for doing certain things well. So if God has given you the ability to prophesy, speak out with as much faith as God has given you. If your gift is serving others, serve them well. If you are a teacher, teach well. If your gift is to encourage others, be encouraging. If it is giving, give generously. If God has given you leadership ability, take the responsibility seriously. And if you have a gift for showing kindness to others, do it gladly." **ROMANS 12:6-8 (NLT)**

Play Offense

"The heart of man plans his way, but the LORD establishes his steps." **PROVERBS 16:9 (ESV)**

"I repeat, be strong and brave! Don't be afraid and don't panic, for I, the LORD your God, am with you in all you do." **JOSHUA 1:9 (NET)**

"Work hard and become a leader; be lazy and become a slave." **PROVERBS 12:24 (NLT)**

Establish a Track Record of Faithfulness

"Whatever you do, work heartily, as for the Lord and not for men." **COLOSSIANS 3:23 (ESV)**

"A wicked messenger falls into trouble, but a faithful envoy brings healing." **PROVERBS 13:17 (ESV)**

"A faithful person will have an abundance of blessings, but the one who hastens to gain riches will not go unpunished." **PROVERBS 28:20 (NET)**

Find the Right Work Teammates

Jesus - He chose a diverse group of talented and faithful men to partner with Him in carrying out His work on Earth. **MATTHEW 4:19**

Paul - He was continuously partnering with teammates as he was focused on building the early church. **2 TIMOTHY 2:2, GALATIANS 1:1, PHILIPPIANS 1:1**

King David- He surrounded himself with a valued and trusted team of men that he called his "mighty men." **1 CHRONICLES 28**

Establish a Culture of Encouragement

"Therefore encourage one another and build one another up." **I THESSALONIANS 5:11 (ESV)**

"Let each of you look not only to his own interests, but also to the interests of others." **PHILIPPIANS 2:4 (ESV)**

"Love one another with brotherly affection. Outdo one another in showing honor." **ROMANS 12:10 (ESV)**

Use Your Work-Related Talents To Bless Your Community

"In all things, I have shown you that by working hard, in this way we must help the weak and remember the words of the Lord Jesus, how he himself said, 'it is more blessed to give than to receive.'" **ACTS 20:35 (ESV)**

"When it goes well with the righteous, the city rejoices, and when the wicked parish there are shouts of gladness. By the blessing of the upright a city is exalted, but by the mouth of the wicked it is overthrown." **PROVERBS 11:10-11 (ESV)**

"But seek the welfare of the city where I have sent you into exile, and pray to the LORD on its behalf, for in its welfare you will find your welfare." **JEREMIAH 29:7 (ESV)**

USE YOUR **WORK-RELATED TALENTS** TO

Bless your Community

FORMER NFL TIGHT-END KEITH JACKSON IS ONE BUSY GUY, YET STILL FINDS TIME TO USE HIS SKILLS TO SERVE THE COMMUNITY.

While Keith Jackson feels blessed to have had an exciting NFL career with the Philadelphia Eagles, Miami Dolphins, and Green Bay Packers, he is even more excited about embracing opportunities to bless his community.

Since retiring from the NFL, Keith's work-life has taken him in a number of different directions. He travels frequently as a much-in-demand speaker, serves as the color commentator for college football games, is TV spokesman for a variety of businesses and is a successful entrepreneur in his own right. As busy as he is, he makes it a priority to use his work-related talents to bless others and make a difference in his community.

In addition to all of his work responsibilities, Keith founded and leads a program (P.A.R.K. – Positive Atmosphere Reaches Kids) that, He applies the same hard work and leadership skills that have made him a successful businessman to the PARK program.

His willingness to share his time and skills with the community has blessed hundreds of kids with a new hope and purpose in life that they never thought could be possible. Hundreds who would have never even thought about the possibility of college have graduated from the PARK program to earn college scholarships. Even better, God is using Keith to point kids to Jesus as the ultimate hope in their lives and then discipling them in His truths.

Keith is a great example of a man who believes that God put him on this earth to do more than just chase success, make money, and pursue power. His goal is to use the talents and skills that God has given him to bless others and bring glory to God in his community. May his example inspire all of us to use the skills we've developed in our careers to bless our communities outside of our work-lives.

"WELL

"The book of Genesis leaves us with a striking truth -- work was part of paradise."
Tim Keller

"If you're changing the world, you're working on important things. You're excited to get up in the morning."
Larry Page, CEO of Google

"If people knew how hard I had to work to gain my mastery, it would not seem so wonderful at all." *Michelangelo*

"Since we already have in Christ the things other people work for --- salvation, self-worth, a good conscience, and peace --- now we may work simply to love God and our neighbors." *Tim Keller*

"Your daily work is ultimately an act of worship to the God who called and equipped you to do it -- no matter what kind of work it is." *Tim Keller*

"Any man can work when every stroke of his hands brings down the fruit rattling from the tree but to labor in season and out of season, under every discouragement... that requires a heroism which is transcendent."
Henry Ward Beecher

SAID

"Pray as though everything depended on God. Work as though everything depended on you." *Augustine*

"All labor that uplifts humanity has dignity and importance and should be undertaken with painstaking excellence." *Martin Luther King, Jr.*

"The good news (or gospel) of Christ turns our lives and the way we work upside down." *Tim Keller*

"Opportunity is missed by most people because it is dressed in overalls and looks like work." *Thomas A. Edison*

"Success is a lousy teacher. It seduces smart people into thinking they can't lose." *Bill Gates*

"The average person puts only 25% of his energy and ability into his work." *Andrew Carnegie*

"The question regarding our choice of work is no longer 'What will make me the most money and give me the most status?' The question must now be 'How, with my existing abilities and opportunities, can I be of greatest service to other people?'" *Tim Keller*

WORK IN THE SPIRIT - TOWARD A THEOLOGY OF WORK

By Miroslave Volf

Although there have been many popular books on the Christian understanding of work, this is the first scholarly effort to articulate a developed Protestant theology. Volf interprets work from a new perspective--in terms of the doctrine of the Holy Spirit--and explores the nature of work in both capitalist and socialist societies.

HOW THEN SHOULD WE WORK?

By Hugh Whelchel

Many Christians struggle to make sense of their faith and work. Some are taught the only value in their work is evangelism among their coworkers and earning money to donate to the church and missions. With more than 25 years working in the business sector, Hugh Whelchel was just that guy. He knew there had to be more. His thorough investigation reveals the eternal significance of work within the grand, Biblical story of God's mission throughout history.

BUSINESS FOR THE GLORY OF GOD

By Wayne Grudem

Wayne Grudem introduces a novel concept: business itself glorifies God when it is conducted in a way that imitates God's character and creation. He shows that all aspects of business, including ownership, profit, money, competition, and borrowing and lending, glorify God because they are reflective of God's nature. Though Grudem isn't naïve about the easy ways these activities can be perverted and used as a means to sin, he knows that Christians can be about the business of business.

KINGDOM CALLING

By Amy Sherman

Amy Sherman, director of the Center on Faith in Communities and scholar of vocational stewardship, uses the "tsaddiqim"- the people who see everything they have as gifts from God to be stewarded for his purposes-- as a springboard to explore how, through our faith-formed calling, we announce the kingdom of God to our everyday world.

ALL LABOR HAS DIGNITY

By Martin Luther King, Jr.

Gathered in one volume for the first time, the majority of these speeches will be new to most readers. The collection begins with King's lectures to unions in the 1960s and includes his addresses made during his Poor People's Campaign, culminating with his momentous "Mountaintop" speech, delivered in support of striking black sanitation workers in Memphis. Unprecedented and timely, "All Labor Has Dignity" will more fully restore our understanding of King's lasting vision of economic justice, bringing his demand for equality right into the present.

THE MIND OF THE MAKER

By Dorothy Sayers

Dorothy Sayers sheds new, unexpected light on a specific set of statements made in the Christian creeds. She examines anew such ideas as the image of God, the Trinity, free will, and evil, and in these pages a wholly revitalized understanding of them emerges. The author finds the key in the parallels between the creation of God and the human creative process.

THE OTHER SIX DAYS - VOCATION, WORK AND MINISTRY IN BIBLICAL PERSPECTIV

By R. Paul Stevens

In this provocative book, R. Paul Stevens shows that the clergy-laity division has no basis in the New Testament and challenges all Christians to rediscover what it means to live daily as God's people.

Exploring the theological, structural, and cultural reasons for treating laypeople as the objects of ministry, Stevens argues against the idea of clericalism. All Christians are called to live in faith, hope, and love, and to do God's work in the church and world. This biblical perspective has serious implications for the existing attitudes and practices of many churches as well as for our understanding of ministry. Stevens shows that the task of churches today is to equip people for ministry in their homes, workplaces, and neighborhoods.

RESOURCES

THE CALL - FINDING AND FULFILLING THE CENTRAL PURPOSE OF YOUR LIFE By Os Guinness

The Call continues to stand as a classic, reflective work on life's purpose. Best-selling author Os Guinness goes beyond our surface understanding of God's call and addresses the fact that God has a specific calling for our individual lives.

Why am I here? What is God's call in my life? How do I fit God's call with my own individuality? How should God's calling affect my career, my plans for the future, my concepts of success? Guinness now helps the reader discover answers to these questions, and more, through a corresponding workbook - perfect for individual or group study.

EVERY GOOD ENDEAVOR

By Timothy Keller

With deep insight and often surprising advice, Keller shows readers that biblical wisdom is immensely relevant to our questions about our work. In fact, the Christian view of work—that we work to serve others, not ourselves—can provide the foundation of a thriving professional and balanced personal life. Keller shows how excellence, integrity, discipline, creativity, and passion in the workplace can help others and even be considered acts of worship—not just of self-interest.

GOD AT WORK - YOUR CHRISTIAN VOCATION IN ALL OF LIFE
By Gene Edward Veith, Jr.

Unpacking the Bible's teaching on work, Veith helps us to see the meaning in our vocations, the force behind our ethics, and the transformative presence of God in our everyday, ordinary lives.

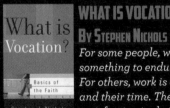

WHAT IS VOCATION?

By Stephen Nichols

For some people, work is tedious and boring, something to endure until the weekend arrives. For others, work is everything; it consumes them and their time. The former find no meaning or satisfaction in their jobs, the latter find too much, both lack an eternal perspective, a biblical framework through which they can evaluate what they spend most of their lives doing.

RESCUING AMBITION
By Dave Harvey

Many think of ambition as nothing more than the drive for personal honor or fame. As a result, ambition—the God-implanted drive to improve, produce, develop, and create—is neglected and well on its way to paralysis.

Dave Harvey is calling for a rescue. He wants to snatch ambition from the heap of failed motivations and put it to work for the glory of God. To understand our ambition, we must understand that we are on a quest for glory. And where we find glory determines the success of our quest.

WORK - A KINGDOM PERSPECTIVE ON LABOR By Ben Witherington III

In this brief primer on the biblical theology and ethics of work, Witherington carefully unpacks the concept of work, considering its relationship to rest, play, worship, the normal cycle of human life, and the coming Kingdom of God. Work as calling, work as ministry, work as a way to make a living, and the notably unbiblical notion of retirement — Witherington's Work engages these subjects and more, combining scholarly acumen with good humor, common sense, cultural awareness, and biblically based insights from Genesis to Revelation.

SCRIPTURE REFERENCES

Proverbs 11:10–11 (NET) "When the righteous do well, the city rejoices ... [and] a city is exalted by the blessing provided from the upright."

Proverbs 11:14 (ESV) "In an abundance of counselors there is safety."

Jeremiah 29:7 (ESV) "Seek the welfare of the city where I have sent you into exile, and pray to the LORD on its behalf, for in its welfare you will find your welfare."

Romans 12:10 (NET) "Be devoted to one another with mutual love, showing eagerness in honoring one another."

1 Corinthians 15:58 (ESV) "Beloved brothers, be steadfast, immovable, always abounding in the work of the Lord, knowing that in the Lord your labor is not in vain."

Colossians 3:23–24 (ESV) "Whatever you do, work heartily, as for the Lord and not for men, knowing that from the Lord you will receive the inheritance as your reward. You are serving the Lord Christ.

Philippians 2:4 (ESV) "Look not only to [your] own interests, but also to the interests of others."

1 Thessalonians 5:11 (ESV) "Encourage one another and build one another up."

1 Peter 4:10–11 (ESV) "As each has received a gift, use it to serve one another, as good stewards of God's varied grace: whoever speaks, as one who speaks oracles of God; whoever serves, as one who serves by the strength that God supplies—in order that in everything God may be glorified through Jesus Christ."

SUPPORTING RESOURCES

Buckingham, Marcus and Donald O. Clifton. *Now Discover Your Strengths*. Free Press. 2001. In this book, which was based on research conducted at Gallup, Buckingham and Clifton argue that individuals should focus on developing their strengths rather than eliminating their weaknesses.

* The content in the resources above does not necessarily reflect the opinion of Authentic Manhood. Readers should utilize these resources but form their own opinions.

ACTION PLAN

YOUR STRATEGIC MOVE | SESSION ONE : **TENSION**

_____

_____

YOUR STRATEGIC MOVE | SESSION TWO : **BLUEPRINT**

_____

_____

YOUR STRATEGIC MOVE | SESSION THREE : **COURAGE**

_____

_____

YOUR STRATEGIC MOVE | SESSION FOUR : **ESSENTIALS**

_____

_____

YOUR STRATEGIC MOVE | SESSION FIVE : **TRAPS**

_____

_____

YOUR STRATEGIC MOVE | SESSION SIX : **CATALYZERS**

_____

_____

ANSWER KEY

A Man and His Work - Answer Key

SESSION ONE: TENSION

I.   2. dominant
      3. process
      5. perspective
II.   1. successful
      3. right
      4.
         • purposeful

III. 1.
         • 71%
      2.
         • satisfied
      3.
         • prioritizing
      4.
         • vision
IV.   1.
         • family
      2.
         • profit
         • dominant
V.   1. leisure
      2.
         • norm
      3.
         • tension
VI   1. deliberate

SESSION TWO: BLUEPRINT

I.   1. Blueprint

II.   1. job
      2.
         • personal
         • mindset
III. 1. modeled
         • created
         • cultivated
      2. imitate
      3. us stewards
         • cultivate
         • develop
         • vision
      4. glory
IV.
      1. image-bearer
         • example
         • follow
      2. life-giving
         • life
      3.
         • humility

SESSION THREE: COURAGE

II.   1. conquered
         • distingished
      2. creator
         • vision
         • life
         • prayer
         •end
      3. cultivator
         • resistance
         • rest
III. 1. life-giving
      2.
         1. ourselves
         3. need
            • giving

SESSION FOUR: ESSENTIALS

II.   1. *gospel*
- *inspires*

2. *best*

3.
- *unique*
- *influence*

4.
- *me*
- *threatened*

5.
- *Resistance*
- *warrior*

6.
- *destroy*

7.
- *pride*
- *redeemed*

8.
- *go get*

9.
- *courage*

10.
- *off*

SESSION FIVE: TRAPS

II.   1. *Unrealistic*
- *dissapointment*
- *biblical*

2.
- *main source*
- *foundation*

3.
    ° *satisfy*
- *borrows*
- *bad*
    ° *love*
    ° *hope*

4.
- *faith*

5.
- *lust*
- *double*

6.
- *goal*
- *season*

SESSION SIX: CATALYZERS

II.   1.
- *not*
- *good*
    ° *coaches*
- *energized*

2. *offense*
- *stuck*

3. *faithfulness*
- *life-giving*
- *Gospel*

4.
- *Paul*

5.
- *life-giving*

6.
- *skill-set*
- *calling*

authenticmanhood.com

- Regular blogs that offer insights and invite conversation
- Other volumes of *33 The Series*
- *Men's Fraternity Classic* and *33 The Series* mobile apps
- Online video and audio downloads
- "Share Your Story" with others
- *Men's Fraternity Classic* curriculum

Join the conversation

facebook facebook.com/33theseries
twitter @33theseries